BUILD OR **DESTROY**
VOLUME 2

"MORE THAN MOTIVATIONAL DOPE"
26 Lessons on Leverage

ANTHONY R. BARBER JR

Dedicated to:
My sons.... "Sabastian & Amari"

CONTENTS

BUILD OR
DESTROY
VOLUME 2

INTRODUCTION
BUILDERS ARE MADE

WELCOME, DEAR READER, to a unique and transformative experience. A lot of time has passed since we last had a conversation, this being Vol.2 of the series I don't plan on disappointing. This is not your typical motivational, self-help book. No, this is a guide that delves deeper into the essence of who you are and explores the boundless potential that lies within you. This is Vol. 2: Let's get started—an invitation to embark on a journey of growth and expansion. In a world saturated with self-help literature, it's easy to feel overwhelmed by the multitude of books promising instant success, happiness, and fulfillment. Yet, amidst this sea of generic advice, there exists a genuine desire within us all to break free from the monotony and limitations of our current lives. We yearn for something more—an opportunity to transcend our perceived boundaries and uncover the extraordinary within. I, Anthony Ronnell Barber Jr (The Builder), stand before you not as an infallible guru with all the answers, but as a fellow traveler on this path of self-discovery. I, too, have felt the weight of self-doubt, the frustration of stagnation, and the fear of never realizing my dreams. However, through the crucible of my own experiences, I have uncovered the transformative power of grinding—the unwavering commitment to personal growth and the relentless pursuit of excellence.

This is a book about more than just motivating you to chase after lofty goals or overcome temporary setbacks. It's about embracing a mindset that transcends momentary inspiration and instead cultivates lasting change. It's about unveiling the true depth of your potential and propelling yourself towards a life of purpose and fulfillment. The pages that lie ahead are not filled with quick fixes or empty promises. Instead, they contain a roadmap for your personal evolution. We will navigate the intricacies of setting achievable goals, conquering the crippling grip of self-doubt, and igniting the fire of motivation even in the face of adversity. What sets this guide apart is its focus on the essence of your being—the core elements that make you unique. While external accomplishments and material success may be worthy pursuits, true growth and expansion stem from an intimate understanding of oneself. It is within this understanding that the seeds of greatness are sown, and the foundation for a truly fulfilling life is built.

Through my own personal stories, triumphs, and failures, I will illustrate the power of resilience, the significance of embracing failure as a steppingstone, and the profound impact of a growth mindset. You will witness firsthand that transformation is not a destination but an ongoing process of continuous evolution towards your highest potential. So, my fellow traveler, if you are ready to embark on a journey of self-discovery, growth, and expansion, then join me. Together, let us delve into the depths of our souls unleash our latent greatness, and build a life that resonates with authenticity, purpose, and success. This is not just another motivational book; it is an invitation to transform your very existence. Are you ready? Let's get started.

LESSON NO. 1
MAKE FRIENDS WITH PAIN

Pain:

"Beast to tame, fuels hunger, strengthens resolve, and breeds champions."

—*BUILD.*

PAIN IS AN inevitable part of life. I had to learn this lesson early on, and the earlier you accept this part of life, the more effective you'll be. Early on in my investment journey, I received a lot of backlashes from members of my own race as well as some close family members. They told me that investing was a white man's game, and that I would never be successful. This pain and depression almost made me give up on my dream of becoming a successful investor.

However, I realized that I could either let this pain destroy me, or I could use it as leverage to fuel my success. I decided to double down on my options trading and build up my dividend portfolio. I knew that if I could succeed in this field, it would be a major accomplishment for my race and open new doors for other less fortunate people.

I started to view the pain I was experiencing as a friend. It was a reminder of my purpose and what I was fighting for. It was also a motivator to keep going, even when things were tough.

I eventually became successful in my investment journey. I was able to break down stereotypes and open new doors for others. I learned that pain is not something to be avoided. It is something to be embraced and used as leverage to achieve your goals.

Here are some tips on how to make friends with pain:

- Acknowledge the pain. The first step to making friends with pain is to acknowledge it. Don't try to ignore it or pretend it doesn't exist.

- Understand the purpose of the pain. What is the pain trying to tell you? What is it trying to teach you?

- Use the pain as motivation. Let the pain fuel your fire and motivate you to keep going.

- Don't let the pain control you. You are in control of your own destiny. Don't let the pain dictate your actions.

Pain is a part of life. It is something that we all experience at some point. However, we don't have to let pain destroy us. We can use it as leverage to achieve our goals and make a difference in the world.

In the context of the book, this lesson teaches us that we can use the pain and challenges we face in life as an opportunity to grow and become stronger. We can also use them to fuel our success and make a difference in the world.

We all experience physical, emotional, and mental pain at some point in our lives. However, it's not the pain itself that defines us but how we choose to respond to it. In this chapter, we will explore the power of pain as it relates to resilience, and how it can be harnessed to help us overcome adversity and achieve success. Resilience is the ability to bounce back from adversity and overcome challenges. It's the ability to persevere in the face of pain, failure, and setbacks. And while resilience is often associated with strength and toughness, it's important to recognize that it's not something that comes naturally to everyone. In fact, resilience is often born out of pain and suffering. Pain can be a powerful motivator. It can push us to our limits and help us discover our true strength and resilience. When we experience pain, we have a choice. We can either succumb to it or use it as fuel to propel us forward. And it's this choice that defines our resilience.

Let's take the story of Nick Vujicic, for example. Nick was born without arms and legs, a condition known as tetra-Amelia syndrome. Growing up, he faced intense physical and emotional pain, as he struggled to fit in with his peers and navigate the challenges of everyday life. However, instead of succumbing to his pain and giving up, Nick used it as a motivator to achieve incredible success. He learned to use his feet to perform tasks that others do with their hands, such as typing, writing, and even swimming. He became an inspirational speaker, traveling the world to share his story of resilience and hope with others. Through his experiences, Nick discovered that pain can be a powerful tool for growth and resilience. It's not the absence of pain that makes us strong but our ability to face it head-on and use it to our advantage. By embracing our pain and using it as motivation, we can build the resilience needed to overcome even the toughest challenges.

THE BREAKDOWN:

Pain is a powerful force that can either break us or make us stronger. When we experience pain, we have a choice. We can choose to let it define us or use it to fuel our resilience and achieve success. So, let us embrace our pain, learn from it, and use it as a powerful tool on our grind towards success. When it comes to pain, humans have an innate response known as the fight or flight response. This response is a survival mechanism that's hardwired into our biology and helps us respond to threats in our environment. In this chapter, we will explore how the fight or flight response relates to pain and how we can harness it to build resilience and achieve success. The fight or flight response is triggered by a perceived threat, which could be physical or emotional in nature. When we experience pain, our bodies interpret it as a threat and activate the fight or flight response. This response prepares our bodies to either fight the threat or flee from it.

NOTE: In Physiologically, the fight or flight response involves the release of adrenaline and other stress hormones, which increase our heart rate, blood pressure, and respiration. This response also triggers a range of physical changes, such as increased muscle tension and decreased digestion.

While the fight or flight response is essential for survival in dangerous situations, it can also have negative consequences when it comes to pain. For example, when we experience chronic pain, our bodies may become stuck in a constant state of stress, which can lead to a range of health issues, including anxiety, depression, and cardiovascular disease. However, by understanding the fight or flight response and how it relates to pain, we can use it to our advantage. By recognizing pain as a threat and activating the fight or flight response, we can harness our bodies' natural resilience and build the strength needed to overcome challenges.

For example, if we're experiencing chronic pain, we can use the fight or flight response to motivate us to seek out medical help and find ways to manage our pain. We can also use this response to motivate us to act towards our goals and build resilience in the face of setbacks. The fight or flight response is a natural response to pain that's hardwired into our biology. While it can have negative consequences when it comes to chronic pain, we can also harness it to build resilience and achieve success. By recognizing pain as a threat and using the fight or flight response to our advantage, we can overcome adversity and achieve our goals on our grind towards success.

LESSON NO. 2
THE POWER OF AFFIRMATION

Affirmation:
"Fuel for the mind, igniting belief, and manifesting fortunes. Speak, believe, achieve."

—*BUILD*

As you continue your grind, it's important to keep your mind in a positive state. No, I do not mean forcefully positive, but in a constant state of mind, a sense of knowing on an internal level can be a critical weapon in your daily arsenal of positive self-talk. Affirmations are positive statements that we repeat to ourselves in order to improve our self-esteem and motivation. They can be a powerful tool for changing our mindset and achieving our goals.

Personal story

I learned the power of affirmation from an older gentleman I used to work with named Frank. Frank was a luggage handler for a major airline, and he had been working there for over 30 years. He was a wise and experienced man, and he always had a positive attitude. I was young and new to the job, and I was often feeling overwhelmed and stressed. I would work long hours and I was always in a hurry to clock out. Frank noticed that I was starting to burn out, and he took me aside one day and gave me some advice.

He said, "Young blood, young blood. Why are you in such a hurry to clock out? Every minute gained is a blessing earned. Slow down. "Frank's words made a big impact on me". I realized that I was letting my negative self-talk get the best of me. I was constantly telling myself that I wasn't good enough, and that I would never be successful. Frank's words helped me to change my mindset. I started to repeat positive affirmations to myself, such as "I am capable," "I am worthy," and "I am successful."

The power of affirmation

Affirmations can be a powerful tool for changing our mindset and achieving our goals. When we repeat positive statements to ourselves, we start to believe them. This can lead to several benefits, including:

- Increased self-esteem

- Improved motivation

- Reduced stress

- Increased productivity

- Better decision-making

How to use affirmations

There are a few things to keep in mind when using affirmations:

- Make sure your affirmations are positive and present tense.

- Repeat your affirmations regularly, such as when you wake up, before bed, or during your morning commute.

- Believe in your affirmations, even if you don't believe them at first.

THE BREAKDOWN:

Affirmations are a powerful tool that can help us to change our mindset and achieve our goals. If you are struggling with negative self-talk, I encourage you to try using affirmations. They may just be the key to your success. In the context of the book, this lesson teaches us that we can use our own words to empower ourselves and achieve our goals. We can also use them to overcome negative self-talk and build a positive mindset.

Your mindset can determine your success or failure, and one powerful tool for maintaining a positive mindset is affirmation. Affirmation is a simple yet effective technique of positive self-talk. It involves repeating positive statements to yourself, focusing your mind on positive outcomes and beliefs. By affirming positive thoughts, you can shift your focus from negative self-talk and doubt to confidence and success. Affirmations can help you achieve your goals, no matter how big or small they are. They can boost your self-esteem, help you overcome fear and self-doubt, and increase your resilience when facing challenges. Affirmations can also improve your mental health by reducing stress, anxiety, and depression. To use affirmations effectively, you must believe in them. If you don't believe what you're saying, it won't have the desired effect. Therefore, it's essential to choose affirmations that resonate with you and align with your goals.

Here are some examples of affirmations that you can use:

- I can achieve my goals.

- I have the skills and knowledge to succeed.

- I am confident in myself and my abilities.

- I am resilient and can overcome any obstacle.

- I am worthy of success and happiness.

- I am surrounded by positive and supportive people.

To use affirmations, find a quiet space and repeat them to yourself, preferably in front of a mirror. Speak to them with conviction and belief, as if they are already true. You can also write them down and post them in a visible place to remind yourself throughout the day. Affirmations should be a regular part of your daily routine. Make it a habit to affirm positive thoughts every morning and night. Use them as a tool to combat negative self-talk and replace it with positive self-talk.

In addition to affirmations, visualization is another powerful tool that can help you achieve your goals. Visualization involves creating mental images of what you want to achieve. By visualizing your goals, you can create a clear and compelling picture of what you want to accomplish, and this can help you stay focused and motivated. To visualize effectively, find a quiet space and close your eyes. Imagine yourself achieving your goals in vivid detail, using all your senses. See yourself succeeding, hear success, and feel the emotions of accomplishment.

Visualize yourself living the life you want to live and feel the joy and happiness that comes with it. Affirmation and visualization are powerful tools that can help you achieve your goals and maintain a positive mindset. Use them regularly as a part of your daily routine, and you'll see the positive impact they can have on your life. Remember, you have the power to create the life you want to live, so use these tools to help you get there.

The Mind of a Champion

Let me tell you about the inspiring story of Muhammad Ali, a boxing legend and Olympic gold medalist, who used positive affirmations to overcome self-doubt and become one of the greatest athletes of all time. Ali was born Cassius Clay in Louisville, Kentucky, in 1942. As a child, he struggled with dyslexia and was often ridiculed by his classmates. However, he found solace in boxing, and at the age of 12, he began training with a local police officer. As Ali's boxing career took off, he faced many challenges and setbacks. In 1960, he competed in the Rome Olympics and won a gold medal in the light heavyweight division. However, upon his return to the US, he faced racism and discrimination, despite his Olympic success.

During this time, Ali began to use positive affirmations to combat the negative thoughts and doubts that crept into his mind. He would repeat phrases like "I am the greatest" and "I am the champ" to himself, even before he had won any major titles. In 1964, Ali faced his biggest challenge yet when he was scheduled to fight Sonny Liston, the heavyweight champion of the world. Many people doubted Ali's abilities and thought he was too young and inexperienced to win. However, Ali remained confident and continued to repeat his positive affirmations.

Despite the odds, Ali defeated Liston in a stunning upset and became the heavyweight champion of the world. He continued to use positive affirmations throughout his career, often reciting poems that he had written himself to motivate himself and intimidate his opponents. Ali's positive mindset and unwavering self-belief led him to achieve incredible success in his boxing career. He went on to win three heavyweight titles, become an Olympic gold medalist, and become one of the most recognized and celebrated athletes of all time.

THE BREAKDOWN:

Muhammad Ali's story is a powerful example of how positive affirmations can help us overcome self-doubt and achieve great success. By maintaining a positive mindset and focusing on our goals, we can overcome any obstacle and reach our full potential. So, let us take a page out of Ali's book and use positive affirmations to motivate ourselves on our grind towards success.

The Mind of the Artist

Let me tell you about the tragic story of Vincent van Gogh, a Dutch post-impressionist painter, who struggled with mental illness and received negative affirmations from his family and society, leading to his eventual failure.

Van Gogh was born in 1853 in the Netherlands and initially worked as an art dealer before pursuing his passion for painting. He produced over 2,000 artworks in his lifetime, but his paintings were not well-received during his lifetime. He faced constant criticism and ridicule from his family and the art establishment, who dismissed his work as ugly and unappealing.

As a result of this negative affirmation, van Gogh began to doubt his abilities and suffered from depression and anxiety. He turned to alcohol and suffered several breakdowns, eventually checking himself into a mental asylum. During his time at the asylum, van Gogh continued to paint, but his mental state continued to deteriorate. He suffered from seizures and hallucinations, which he believed enhanced his artistic vision. However, his paintings continued to be dismissed and ridiculed by his family and the art establishment, fueling his self-doubt and despair. In 1890, van Gogh died by suicide at the age of 37, never having achieved commercial success or recognition for his work during his lifetime. It wasn't until after his death that his work was recognized as a groundbreaking contribution to the world of art. Van Gogh's story is a tragic example of how negative affirmation can lead to failure and even tragedy. His constant exposure to negative feedback and criticism led to a negative mindset, self-doubt, and ultimately, his untimely death. Had he received positive affirmation and encouragement for his work, perhaps he could have achieved greater success and recognition during his lifetime.

Vincent van Gogh's story is a stark reminder of the power of negative affirmation and the importance of positive feedback and encouragement. As we strive to achieve our goals and reach our full potential, let us surround ourselves with positive and supportive people who can provide constructive feedback and affirmation to keep us motivated and focused on our grind towards success.

LESSON NO. 3
THE POWER OF GRATITUDE

Gratitude:
"Currency that appreciates in value, unlocking abundance and attracting prosperity."

—*BUILD*

GRATITUDE IS A powerful force that can transform our lives and help us achieve our goals.

When we focus on what we're grateful for, we attract more positive experiences and opportunities into our lives. This is why it's important to leverage gratitude as a tool for success. One way to leverage gratitude is by keeping a gratitude journal. Each day, take a few moments to write down three things that you're grateful for. This could be anything from a good meal to a supportive friend to a successful project at work. By focusing on the good things in your life, you'll start to notice more positive experiences and opportunities.

Another way to leverage gratitude is by expressing appreciation to others. When someone does something kind or helpful for you, take a moment to express your gratitude. This could be a simple thank-you note, a phone call, or a heartfelt conversation. By expressing your appreciation, you'll not only make the other person feel good, but you'll also cultivate a positive relationship that could lead to future opportunities. Gratitude can also help us develop a more positive mindset. When we focus on what we're grateful for, we shift our focus away from negative thoughts and emotions. This can help us develop a more optimistic outlook on life, which can lead to increased resilience, creativity, and problem-solving skills.

Moreover, gratitude can help us build better relationships with others. When we express appreciation and gratitude towards others, we strengthen our connections and build trust. This can lead to more opportunities for collaboration, mentorship, and support. Gratitude can indeed be used as a subtle weapon in various situations. It can be used to disarm a potential opponent or even turn an enemy into an ally. When we express gratitude towards someone, it can create a sense of indebtedness in that person. This indebtedness can then be used to influence their behavior or actions in the future.

Here are some pros and cons of gratitude in terms of business and interpersonal relationships:

Pros:

- Increased productivity: Gratitude can help to increase productivity in the workplace by creating a more positive and supportive environment. When employees feel appreciated, they are more likely to be motivated and engaged in their work.

- Improved teamwork: Gratitude can help to improve teamwork by promoting cooperation and collaboration. When team members feel grateful for each other's contributions, they are more likely to work together effectively and achieve common goals.

- Enhanced customer service: Gratitude can help to enhance customer service by creating a more positive and memorable experience for customers. When customers feel appreciated, they are more likely to be loyal and repeat customers.

- Stronger relationships: Gratitude can help to strengthen relationships by building trust and appreciation. When people feel grateful for each other, they are more likely to be supportive and understanding.

Cons:

- Can be misconstrued: Gratitude can sometimes be misconstrued as weakness or a sign of vulnerability. If not expressed carefully, it can backfire and make the recipient feel uncomfortable.

- Can be seen as insincere: If gratitude is not sincere, it can come across as insincere or manipulative. This can damage relationships and make people less likely to be open to receiving gratitude in the future.

- Can be time-consuming: Expressing gratitude can take time and effort. If not done thoughtfully, it can come across as superficial or forced.

In the context of the book chapter titled "Lesson no. 3 The power of gratitude," the pros of gratitude outweigh the cons. Gratitude is a powerful emotion that can have a positive impact on both business and interpersonal relationships. When expressed sincerely, gratitude can help to create a more positive and productive environment, improve teamwork, enhance customer service, and strengthen relationships.

However, it is important to be mindful of the potential cons of gratitude. Gratitude should not be used to manipulate or take advantage of others. It should also be expressed in a way that is sincere and thoughtful. Overall, gratitude is a powerful emotion that can have a positive impact on our lives. If we are mindful of the potential cons, gratitude can be a valuable tool for building strong relationships and achieving success in business.

For example, imagine you have a colleague who is constantly competing with you for the same promotion or project at work. Instead of responding with aggression or hostility, you could try expressing gratitude towards them for their contributions to the team or for their unique skills and expertise. This could help to shift their perspective and create a sense of goodwill towards you. Similarly, in a business negotiation, expressing gratitude towards the other party can create a sense of goodwill and trust. This can help to build a more positive relationship and increase the likelihood of reaching a mutually beneficial agreement. However, it's important to note that using gratitude as a weapon should never involve insincerity or manipulation. Expressing gratitude should always come from a place of genuine appreciation and respect for the other person. In addition, gratitude should not be used to avoid confrontation or to suppress one's own needs or desires. It should be used as a tool for building positive relationships and achieving mutual goals, rather than to manipulate or control others. Used appropriately, gratitude can be a powerful and subtle tool for building positive relationships and achieving success in various areas of life.

THE BREAKDOWN:

Leveraging gratitude is a powerful tool for success. By keeping a gratitude journal, expressing appreciation to others, cultivating a positive mindset, and building better relationships, we can attract more positive experiences and opportunities into our lives. Gratitude is a key ingredient in the recipe for success, and it's something we can all cultivate and leverage in our daily lives.

LESSON NO. 4
THE STRENGTH OF BONDS

"Harnessing the Power of Friendship
and Networking"

Strong bonds:
"The foundation of success, built with trust, loyalty,
and unbreakable alliances."

—*BUILD*

IN THIS CHAPTER, we dive deep into the extraordinary influence that friendships and networking can have on one's journey to success. Building and nurturing meaningful connections is an essential aspect of personal and professional growth. Join me as we explore historical and recent examples that showcase the power of friendship and networking in a way that will leave you inspired and ready to forge new alliances.

The Ancient Art of Connections As we examine history, we

can find numerous instances where friendships and networks played pivotal roles in shaping destinies.

EXAMPLE 1:

The Alliance of Caesar and Cleopatra: In ancient Rome, Julius Caesar and Cleopatra forged a powerful bond that transcended borders. Their friendship resulted in a strategic alliance that significantly impacted both of their realms, enabling Caesar to gain influence and Cleopatra to solidify her position as the ruler of Egypt. Together, they exemplified the immense power of leveraging friendships to achieve shared goals.

The Medici Family: Patrons of the Renaissance: During the Renaissance, the Medici family in Florence, Italy, cultivated an extensive network of artists, scientists, and thinkers. By fostering these friendships and providing patronage, they fueled the intellectual and artistic revolution of their time. This network of talented individuals transformed Florence into a center of innovation and creativity, leaving an indelible mark on history.

EXAMPLE 2:

Contemporary Connections While historical examples offer valuable insights, the power of friendship and networking remains relevant today. Let's explore recent instances where these bonds have shaped lives and shaped the world: Silicon Valley and the PayPal Mafia: In the late 1990s, a group of individuals came together to create an online payment company called PayPal. This venture not only achieved success but also spawned an influential network known as the "PayPal Mafia." These friendships and collaborations led to the birth of groundbreaking companies like Tesla, SpaceX, LinkedIn, and YouTube. The collective power of their network continues to drive innovation and redefine industries.

Malala Yousafzai and Activism: Malala Yousafzai, a young Pakistani activist, forged deep friendships while advocating for girls' education. Through her friendship with other like-minded individuals, she created a powerful global network that amplified her message and united millions in support of her cause. Together, they have sparked a global movement for education and empowerment, demonstrating how friendship and networking can amplify one's impact.

EXAMPLE 3:

Unlocking Your Network's Potential Now that we've explored historical and recent examples of the power of friendship and networking, it's time to harness this power in our own lives. Here are some key principles to consider:

- Cultivate Genuine Connections: Nurture meaningful relationships based on trust, respect, and shared values. Surround yourself with individuals who inspire and challenge you to grow.

- Offer Value and Support: Be proactive in offering assistance and support to your network. By helping others achieve their goals, you establish yourself as a valuable ally and deepen the bonds of friendship.

- Embrace Diversity: Diversify your network by seeking out individuals from various backgrounds, industries, and perspectives. Embracing diversity enhances creativity, broadens horizons, and opens doors to new opportunities.

THE BREAKDOWN:

Friendships and networks have the potential to be transformative forces in our lives. By drawing inspiration from historical and recent examples, we can understand how forging strong connections can lead to remarkable achievements. As you continue your journey, remember that success often thrives within the tapestry of friendship and networking. Embrace these connections, nurture them, and unleash their power to build the future you desire. Remember, it is within your grasp to build or destroy, and continue to grind towards your goals. The power of friendship and networking can be a catalyst for your success or a hindrance if not utilized wisely. Take heed of the lessons shared in this chapter, for they are the keys to unlocking the doors that lead to greatness.

In the world of grinding, there will be obstacles and setbacks, but with a strong network of friends, mentors, and allies, you will have the support and guidance needed to overcome any challenge. Surround yourself with individuals who share your vision and possess the skills and knowledge that complement your own. Together, you can navigate the treacherous waters of entrepreneurship and rise above the competition.

THE EXTRAS:

Be cautious not to misuse the power of networking. Remember that true friendships are built on trust and mutual respect. Do not approach relationships solely for personal gain or treat others as steppingstones on your path to success. Instead, foster genuine connections and be willing to contribute to the growth and development of those around you. By doing so, you will create a network of individuals who are invested in your success and willing to lend a helping hand when needed. In the ever-evolving landscape of business and entrepreneurship, adaptability is crucial. Stay connected with your network, stay informed about industry trends, and be open to collaboration and innovation. Remember the example set by the Medici family, who thrived by embracing new ideas and supporting the creativity of their network. In a world that rewards innovation, your network can provide the inspiration and resources necessary to stay ahead of the curve.

As you embark on your journey to build or destroy, harness the power of friendship and networking as tools to carve your path to success. Draw inspiration from the alliances forged throughout history and the modern-day success stories that have emerged from collaboration and support. Embrace the strength of these bonds and let them propel you towards greatness. I urge you to build your network, forge meaningful connections, and unlock the untapped potential within your relationships. Together, we can overcome any obstacle, seize every opportunity, and build a future where success is not a mere dream but a tangible reality.

resource. Stay connected with your network, stay informed about industry trends, and be open to collaborations and innovation. Remember the example set by the Medici family, who thrived by embracing new ideas and supporting the creativity of their network. In a world that rewards innovation, your network can provide the inspiration and resources necessary to stay ahead of the curve.

As you embark on your journey to build or develop, harness the power of friendship and networking as tools to elevate your path to success. Draw inspiration from the alliances forged throughout history and the modern-day success stories that have emerged from collaboration and support. Embrace the strength of these bonds and let them propel you towards greatness. I urge you to build your network, forge meaningful connections, and unlock the untapped potential within your relationships. Together, we can overcome any obstacle, seize every opportunity, and build a future where success is no more a dream but a tangible reality.

LESSON NO. 5
INFLUENCE IS THE NEW COCAIN

Influence:
"Currency of kings, manipulating minds, shaping destinies, and commanding the markets."

—*BUILD*

NFLUENCE IS A powerful tool that can be used to build or destroy. In the business world, the ability to influence others can make the difference between success and failure. Whether you're trying to persuade investors to fund your startup, convince customers to buy your product, or motivate employees to work harder, your ability to influence others is key. The power of influence comes from your ability to connect with others and build trust. When people trust you, they're more likely to listen to your ideas and act based on your recommendations. Additionally, when you have influence, you can use it to promote positive change and make a difference in the world. Influence and attention are the new cocaine. In the past, people would do anything for a hit of cocaine. They would risk their health, their relationships, and even their lives. Today, people are doing the same thing for a hit of influence and attention. In the age of social media, influence and attention are the currency of success. If you have influence, you can get people to buy your products, follow your advice, and even vote for you. If you have attention, you can become famous, get rich, and live a life of luxury.

That's why people are so desperate for influence and attention. They know that it can give them everything they've ever wanted. But just like cocaine, influence and attention can be addictive. The more you have, the more you want. And the more you want, the more you're willing to do to get it. Influence and attention can be a powerful drug. They can make you feel like you're on top of the world. But they can also destroy you. If you're not careful, they can lead to addiction, isolation, and even death. So next time you're tempted to chase after influence and attention, remember that they're not worth it. They're just like cocaine. They might feel good in the moment, but they'll eventually destroy you.

Here are some additional thoughts on how influence and attention are like cocaine:

- They're both addictive. Once you get a taste of influence and attention, it's hard to stop wanting more.

- They can both lead to destructive behavior. People who are addicted to influence and attention may be willing to do anything to get their next fix. This can lead to risky behavior, such as cyberbullying, trolling, and even violence.

- They can both have serious consequences. Addiction to influence and attention can lead to isolation, depression, and even suicide.

If you're struggling with an addiction to influence and attention, there is help available. There are many resources that can help you learn how to manage your addiction and live a healthy, balanced life.

There are several strategies you can use to develop your influence.

- First, it's important to focus on building strong relationships. This means taking the time to get to know people, understanding their needs and interests, and finding common ground. When you have strong relationships, people are more likely to listen to your ideas and act based on your recommendations.

- Second, it's important to be an effective communicator. This means being clear, concise, and confident when you speak. Additionally, you should be able to listen actively and respond to feedback in a constructive way. When you're an effective communicator, people are more likely to trust and respect you, which can increase your influence.

- Third, it's important to lead by example. This means demonstrating your values and principles through your actions. When you lead by example, you inspire others to follow your lead and adopt your values and principles.

THE BREAKDOWN:

The power of influence is a valuable tool that can help you achieve your goals and make a positive impact on the world. By focusing on building strong relationships, being an effective communicator, leading by example, and being authentic, you can develop your influence and use it to build rather than destroy. Being influential is a powerful feeling that can be addictive for many people. When you can influence others, you have the power to make a real difference in the world and bring about change. However, with this power comes a great responsibility to use it wisely and ethically. One reason why being influential can be addictive is because it gives people a sense of purpose and meaning. When you can influence others, you feel like you are making a difference and contributing to something greater than yourself. This can be incredibly fulfilling and rewarding, which can make it hard to give up.

Another reason why being influential can be addictive is because it can lead to more opportunities and rewards. When you have a large following or a significant amount of influence, you may be approached with more opportunities for business partnerships, speaking engagements, and other types of collaborations. These opportunities can bring financial rewards and other benefits, which can further reinforce the addictive nature of influence. However, it's important to remember that influence can also be a double-edged sword. While it can bring about positive change and opportunities, it can also be misused and lead to negative consequences. Influence can be used to manipulate and exploit others, which can ultimately lead to a loss of trust and credibility. To use influence in a positive way, it's important to focus on building relationships and creating value for others. This means being transparent, ethical, and authentic in your interactions with others. It also means using your influence to bring about positive change and make a meaningful impact on the world. Being influential can be addictive for many people because it provides a sense of purpose, meaning, and opportunity. However, it's important to use influence in an ethical and responsible way, focusing on building relationships and creating value for others. By doing so, you can use your influence to bring about positive change and make a lasting impact on the world.

THE BREAKDOWN (NEGATIVE):

One example of influence backfiring in a negative way is the case of Richard Nixon, the 37th President of the United States. Nixon was a highly influential politician who served as President from 1969 to 1974. However, his influence became his undoing when he was implicated in the Watergate scandal.

- In 1972, during Nixon's re-election campaign, five men were caught breaking into the Democratic National Committee headquarters at the Watergate complex in Washington D.C. The Nixon administration was initially able to distance itself from the incident, but as the investigation deepened, evidence emerged that Nixon himself had been involved in a cover-up.

- In August 1974, Nixon resigned from office in the face of almost certain impeachment and removal from office. His downfall was the result of his desire to maintain his influence and power at all costs, which ultimately led him to engage in unethical and illegal activities.

The example of Nixon illustrates how being influential can become addictive and lead to a desire to maintain that influence at any cost. However, when that desire for power and influence is pursued through unethical or illegal means, it can lead to catastrophic consequences, both for the individual and for those around them. It is important to remember that influence and power should be wielded responsibly and with an eye towards ethical behavior.

THE BREAK DOWN (POSITIVE):

One example of addictive influence having a positive impact is the story of Mahatma Gandhi, the leader of the Indian independence movement against British rule in the early to mid-20th century. Gandhi was a highly influential figure in Indian society, and his nonviolent methods of protest and civil disobedience helped inspire a generation of activists and leaders around the world. Gandhi's influence was the result of his unwavering commitment to his principles of nonviolence, truthfulness, and self-discipline. He was able to build a massive following of supporters who were willing to follow him to the ends of the earth in pursuit of Indian independence. Even when faced with violence and oppression from the British authorities, Gandhi remained steadfast in his commitment to nonviolent resistance. Gandhi's influence was addictive not because he craved power or control, but because he was driven by a deep sense of purpose and conviction. He saw his struggle for Indian independence as part of a larger movement towards justice and equality for all people, and he was willing to sacrifice his own well-being for the sake of that cause. Gandhi's legacy continues to inspire people around the world to this day. His message of nonviolence and his unwavering commitment to his principles serve as a reminder that influence can be a force for good when it is used to advance noble causes and promote positive change.

LESSON NO. 6
THE IMPORTANCE OF TEACHING CHILDREN
CODING, STEM, FUTURE SKILLS

Teaching:
"Weapon of wisdom, empowering minds, and creating an army of unstoppable achievers."

—BUILD

IN TODAY'S DIGITAL age, technology is advancing at an incredible pace, and it's becoming increasingly important for children to learn coding and STEM skills. In this chapter, we'll explore why teaching children how to code or STEM is so important and how you can get started.

Here is a breakdown of the importance of exposing children to skilled trades and STEM from an early age:

- Skilled trades are in high demand. The demand for skilled trades workers is growing, and is expected to continue to grow in the coming years. This is due to several factors, including the aging workforce, the increasing complexity of technology, and the need for skilled workers in new and emerging industries.

- STEM careers are also in high demand. STEM careers are those that involve science, technology, engineering, and mathematics. These careers are also growing in demand, due to the increasing importance of technology in our society.

- Exposing children to skilled trades and STEM from an early age can help them develop the skills they need to succeed in these fields. This can be done by taking them to trade shows, visiting construction sites, or even just letting them explore their own interests.

- Exposing children to skilled trades and STEM can also help them develop a strong work ethic and problem-solving skills. These are essential skills for success in any field.

- Finally, exposing children to skilled trades and STEM can help them develop a sense of pride and accomplishment. This can be a great motivator for children and can help them stay on track to achieve their goals.

Here are some specific benefits of exposing children to skilled trades and STEM from an early age:

- They can learn valuable skills that will help them get good-paying jobs.

- They can develop a strong work ethic and problem-solving skills.

- They can learn about different career options and find something that they are passionate about.

- They can gain confidence and self-esteem.

- They can make new friends and connections.

If you are interested in exposing your child to skilled trades and STEM, there are a few things you can do:

- Talk to your child about your own experiences with these fields.

- Take your child to trade shows, construction sites, or other events where they can learn more about these fields.

- Encourage your child to explore their own interests and hobbies.

- Help your child find mentors or role models who work in these fields.

- Support your child's education and learning.

Exposing children to skilled trades and STEM from an early age can give them a head start in life and help them achieve their full potential.

Why is Teaching Children How to Code or STEM Important?

Here are a few reasons why teaching children how to code or STEM is so important:

- Job Opportunities: With technology playing an increasingly central role in our lives, there is a growing demand for workers with coding and STEM skills. By learning these skills at a young age, children can position themselves for future job opportunities and career success.

- Critical Thinking Skills: Learning to code or STEM can help children develop critical thinking skills, problem-solving abilities, and logical reasoning skills. These skills can benefit them in all areas of life and lead to greater success in school and beyond.

- Creativity: Coding and STEM skills can also foster creativity, as children are encouraged to think outside the box and come up with innovative solutions to problems.

- Digital Literacy: In today's world, digital literacy is becoming increasingly important. By learning coding and STEM skills, children can develop a deeper understanding of how technology works and how to navigate the digital landscape safely and responsibly.

How to Teach Children How to Code or STEM

If you're interested in teaching your children how to code or STEM, here are a few tips to help you get started:

- Start Early: It's never too early to start teaching children how to code or STEM. Even young children can learn basic concepts through games, toys, and simple programming languages like Scratch.

- Make it Fun: Learning to code or STEM doesn't have to be boring. Look for interactive games, puzzles, and other activities that make learning fun and engaging.

- Encourage Experimentation: Coding and STEM skills are all about experimentation and trial and error. Encourage children to experiment and try new things, even if they fail at first.

- Find Resources: There are many resources available to help parents teach their children how to code or STEM, including online courses, books, and educational programs.

THE BREAKDOWN:

In addition to these benefits, STEM education can also help children develop a better understanding of the world around them. This is important in the age of artificial intelligence (AI), as AI is becoming increasingly prevalent in our lives.

For example, children who are exposed to STEM education at a young age will be better equipped to understand how AI works and how it can be used to solve problems. They will also be better equipped to critically evaluate the claims made about AI and to make informed decisions about how to use AI in their own lives.

Overall, STEM education can provide children with a number of benefits that will help them succeed in the new technology age. These benefits include critical thinking and problem-solving skills, curiosity, creativity and innovation, teamwork skills, and a better understanding of the world around them.

Here are some specific examples of how children born into the new technology age will benefit from STEM education:

- They will be able to understand how AI works and how it can be used to solve problems. This will give them a competitive edge in the workforce, as AI is becoming increasingly important in many industries.

- They will be able to critically evaluate the claims made about AI and to make informed decisions about how to use AI in their own lives. This will help them avoid being misled by false or misleading information about AI.

- They will be able to use AI to create new and innovative products and services. This will give them the opportunity to make a real difference in the world.

STEM education is essential for children born into the new technology age. It will give them the skills they need to succeed in the workforce, to critically evaluate AI, and to use AI to create new and innovative products and services. Teaching children how to code or STEM is becoming increasingly important in today's digital age. By providing children with these skills, they can position themselves for future job opportunities, develop critical thinking and problem-solving abilities, foster creativity, and develop digital literacy. So, whether you're a parent, teacher, or caregiver, consider introducing coding or STEM to the children in your life and help them build a foundation for success. Remember, teaching children how to code or STEM is just another way of grinding towards success.

LESSON NO. 7
THE POWER OF COMMUNITY

BUILDING A COMMUNITY around your ideas is a powerful way to create a movement and bring about real change. Whether you're an entrepreneur, artist, or activist, building a community can help you to achieve your goals and make a meaningful impact on the world. The first step in building a community is to define your mission and values. What do you stand for, and what do you want to achieve? By defining your mission and values, you can attract like-minded individuals who share your vision and are eager to join your cause. Once you've defined your mission and values, it's important to find ways to connect with others who share your interests. This can include attending events, joining online groups, and reaching out to individuals who are already active in your community. As you begin to connect with others, it's important to create a space where people feel welcome and valued. This can include everything from hosting events and meetups to creating an online forum where people can share ideas and collaborate on projects.

Building a community also requires a commitment to transparency and accountability. It's important to be honest and upfront with your community about your goals and the progress you're making. It's also important to hold yourself and your community accountable for the actions you take and the impact you have on others. Finally, it's important to recognize and celebrate the achievements of your community members. Whether it's recognizing individual accomplishments or celebrating milestones as a group, recognizing and celebrating success can help to build morale and keep your community engaged and motivated. Humans are social creatures. We crave connection and belonging. We need to feel like we are part of something bigger than ourselves. This is why community is so important. A community is a group of people who share common interests or goals. They come together to support each other, learn from each other, and grow together. Communities can be found in all shapes and sizes. They can be based on geography, shared interests, or even shared values.

In modern times, social media has made it easier than ever to connect with others who share our interests. Platforms like Instagram, Twitter, and Facebook allow us to connect with people from all over the world. We can share our thoughts and experiences, and we can learn from others.

social media can be a powerful tool for building community. However, it is important to use it wisely. Social media can also be used to spread hate and division. It is important to be aware of the potential dangers of social media, and to use it in a way that is positive and constructive.

Digital Tribalism

In recent years, there has been a growing trend of digital tribalism. This is the tendency for people to form online communities that are based on shared beliefs and values. These communities can be a source of support and belonging, but they can also be a breeding ground for extremism and hate.

There are several factors that have contributed to the rise of digital tribalism. One factor is the increasing polarization of society. People are increasingly divided along political, religious, and social lines. This polarization makes it easier for people to find others who share their views, and it makes it more difficult for people to understand and empathize with those who hold different views. Another factor that has contributed to the rise of digital tribalism is the anonymity that social media provides. When people are anonymous, they are more likely to say things that they would not say in person. This can lead to an increase in inflammatory rhetoric and hate speech. The rise of digital tribalism is a worrying trend. It has the potential to divide society even further, and it can make it more difficult to find common ground. It is important to be aware of the dangers of digital tribalism, and to use social media in a way that is positive and constructive.

How to Use social media to Build Positive Community... (It's all branding).

There are a few things that you can do to use social media to build positive community. Here are a few tips:

<u>Be mindful of the content that you share</u>: Think about how your words and actions might affect others. Avoid sharing content that is hateful, divisive, or harmful.

<u>Be respectful of others, even if you disagree with them</u>.

Remember that everyone is entitled to their own opinion. Try to understand where others are coming from and be willing to listen to their point of view.

<u>Be positive and encouraging</u>. Focus on the good in people and celebrate their successes. This will help to create a more positive and supportive environment.

<u>Be active in your community.</u> Participate in discussions, share your thoughts and experiences, and offer support to others. This will help to build stronger relationships and create a more vibrant community. Social media can be a powerful tool for building a positive community. By following these tips, you can help to create a more positive and supportive online environment.

THE BREAKDOWN:

Building a community around your ideas is a powerful way to bring about change and achieve your goals. By defining your mission and values, connecting with like-minded individuals, creating a welcoming space, being transparent and accountable, and celebrating success, you can create a movement that has the power to transform lives and make a lasting impact on the world.

LESSON NO. 8
THE IMPORTANCE OF DEVELOPING PATIENCE

Patience:
"The art of restraint, where fortunes align, and the vigilance prevail in due time."

—*BUILD*

IN OUR FAST-PACED society, patience is often seen as a weakness. We're constantly bombarded with messages telling us to "hurry up" and "get things done quickly." However, developing patience is a crucial part of achieving success in any area of life. In this chapter, we'll explore the importance of patience and how you can develop this essential trait. For this well be drawing from one of my favorite historical masterminds…" Hannibal".

Hannibal was a Carthaginian general and military commander who is considered one of the greatest military minds in history. He was born in what is now Tunisia, North Africa, in 247 BC. Hannibal's father, Hamilcar Barca, was a famous Carthaginian general who fought in the First Punic War against Rome. Hannibal followed in his father's footsteps and became a skilled military commander.

Here are some of Hannibal's key characteristics:

- Brave: Hannibal was known for his bravery and his willingness to take risks.

- Strategic: Hannibal was a brilliant strategist and tactician. He was able to outmaneuver his opponents and win battles against superior forces.

- Patient: Hannibal was patient and willing to wait for the right opportunity. He was not afraid to bide his time and let his enemies make mistakes.

- Charismatic: Hannibal was a charismatic leader who was able to inspire his troops to fight for him.

Hannibal was a complex and fascinating figure. He was a brilliant military commander, but he was also a ruthless and ambitious leader. He was a master of strategy and tactics, but he was also willing to take risks and gamble on victory. Still, we shall remain focused on his standout trait, that being his patience.

The Battle of Cannae

The Battle of Cannae was a major battle of the Second Punic War between the Carthaginians and the Romans in 216 BC. The Carthaginians were led by Hannibal, while the Romans were led by Paullus Aemilius.

The battle took place near the town of Cannae in southern Italy. The Carthaginians outnumbered the Romans by a significant margin, but they were able to use their superior patience to win the battle. Hannibal knew that he could not defeat the Romans in a head-on battle. So, he devised a plan to lure the Romans into a trap. He positioned his forces in a crescent formation, with the Romans in the middle. The Romans charged at the Carthaginians, but they were met with a wall of spears. The Carthaginians held their ground, and the Romans were unable to break through. As the Romans became more and more frustrated, Hannibal ordered his forces to slowly withdraw. The Romans followed, eager to finally defeat the Carthaginians. However, as the Romans followed the Carthaginians, they were drawn deeper and deeper into the crescent formation. Eventually, the Romans were surrounded, and they were slaughtered.

The Battle of Cannae was a major victory for the Carthaginians. It showed the importance of patience in war. By being patient, Hannibal was able to lure the Romans into a trap and defeat them in a decisive battle.

Here are some additional details about the Battle of Cannae:

- The battle lasted for about six hours.

- The Carthaginians killed over 50,000 Romans, while the Carthaginians lost only about 6,000 men.

- The Battle of Cannae is considered one of the greatest military victories in history.

The Battle of Cannae teaches us that patience can be a powerful weapon in war. By being patient, we can lure our enemies into traps and defeat them in decisive battles. why Hannibal's patience was a strength in war and strategy:

- It allowed him to see the bigger picture. Hannibal was able to see the long-term implications of his actions, and he was not afraid to make sacrifices in the short-term in order to achieve his long-term goals.

- It allowed him to wait for the right opportunity. Hannibal was not afraid to wait for the right moment to strike. He was willing to bide his time and let his enemies make mistakes.

- It allowed him to stay calm under pressure. Hannibal was able to stay calm and focused even on the heat of battle. This allowed him to make sound decisions and to avoid making mistakes.

- It allowed him to learn from his mistakes. Hannibal was not afraid to admit when he made a mistake. He was able to learn from his mistakes and to improve his strategy.

Overall, Hannibal's patience was a major strength in war and strategy. It allowed him to see the bigger picture, wait for the right opportunity, stay calm under pressure, and learn from his mistakes. These qualities made him one of the greatest military commanders in history.

Here are some specific examples of how Hannibal's patience was used to his advantage in battle:

- The Battle of Cannae: Hannibal knew that he could not defeat the Romans in a head-on battle. So, he devised a plan to lure the Romans into a trap. He positioned his forces in a crescent formation, with the Romans in the middle. He then waited patiently for the Romans to charge. As the Romans became more and more frustrated, Hannibal ordered his forces to slowly withdraw. The Romans followed, eager to finally defeat the Carthaginians. However, as the Romans followed the Carthaginians, they were drawn deeper and deeper into the crescent formation. Eventually, the Romans were surrounded, and they were slaughtered.

- The Siege of Syracuse: Hannibal besieged Syracuse for two years. He knew that he could not take the city by force, so he waited patiently for the city to surrender. Eventually, the Syracusans were forced to surrender due to starvation.

These are just a few examples of how Hannibal's patience was used to his advantage in battle. His patience was a major factor in his success as a military commander.

Why is Patience Important?

- Success Takes Time: Achieving success in any area of life takes time and effort. Whether you're building a business, learning a new skill, or working towards a personal goal, it's important to be patient and understand that success doesn't happen overnight.

- Avoid Burnout: When we're constantly in a rush to get things done, it's easy to become burned out. Developing patience allows us to slow down and take the time we need to recharge and prevent burnout.

- Improved Decision Making: When we're patient, we're able to make better decisions. We're not rushing to make a choice or taking shortcuts. We're taking the time to carefully consider all our options and make the best decision possible.

How to Develop Patience

- Practice Mindfulness: Mindfulness can help you develop patience by allowing you to focus on the present moment and become more aware of your thoughts and feelings. When you're mindful, you're able to slow down and take the time you need to make decisions.

- Set Realistic Expectations: One of the main reasons we become impatient is that we set unrealistic expectations for ourselves. It's important to set goals that are challenging but achievable so that we're not constantly feeling like we're falling behind.

- Embrace the Journey: When we're impatient, we're often focused solely on the result. However, it's important to embrace the journey and enjoy the process of working towards our goals.

- Practice Gratitude: Gratitude can help us develop patience by allowing us to focus on what we have rather than what we lack. When we're grateful, we're able to appreciate the journey and find joy in the small moments.

THE BREAKDOWN:

Developing patience is essential if you want to achieve success in any area of life. By understanding that success takes time, avoiding burnout, and making better decisions, you'll be able to reap the benefits of developing this essential trait. To develop patience, you can practice mindfulness, set realistic expectations, embrace the journey, and practice gratitude. Remember, developing patience is a process, and it won't happen overnight. But with time and practice, you'll be able to cultivate the patience needed to grind towards success.

LESSON NO. 9
REMAINING STOIC

Stoicism:
"The armor of the mind, shielding emotions,
embracing clarity, and seizing control of destiny."

—BUILD

I N LIFE, WE all face adversity at some point. It's how we deal with that adversity that sets us apart. In this chapter, we'll explore the concept of stoicism and why it's important to develop a stoic mindset to face adversity.

What is Stoicism?

Stoicism is a philosophy that originated in ancient Greece and was founded by the philosopher, Zeno. The central idea of stoicism is that we should focus on what is under our control and accept what is not. It's about developing a calm and rational mindset, even in the face of adversity.

Why is Being Stoic Important?

Here are a few reasons why being stoic is so important when facing adversity:

- Emotional Regulation: Being stoic allows us to regulate our emotions and maintain a calm and rational mindset, even in the face of adversity. This can help us avoid making impulsive decisions or reacting in ways that could make the situation worse.

- Resilience: A stoic mindset can help us build resilience and cope with difficult situations. By accepting what we cannot control and focusing on what we can, we can find ways to overcome adversity and grow stronger as a result.

- Clarity of Thought: When we're faced with adversity, it can be difficult to see things clearly. A stoic mindset allows us to step back and assess the situation objectively, which can help us make better decisions and find solutions to the problem at hand.

How to Develop a Stoic Mindset

If you're interested in developing a stoic mindset, here are a few tips to help you get started:

- Focus on What You Can Control: When facing adversity, it's important to focus on what you can control. This includes your thoughts, feelings, and actions. By accepting what you cannot control and focusing on what you can, you can maintain a sense of control over the situation.

- Practice Mindfulness: Mindfulness can help you develop a stoic mindset by allowing you to focus on the present moment and become more aware of your thoughts and emotions. This can help you regulate your emotions and maintain a calm and rational mindset.

- Embrace Discomfort: Adversity can be uncomfortable, but embracing discomfort can help you build resilience and develop a stoic mindset. By pushing yourself outside of your comfort zone, you can learn to tolerate discomfort and develop the mental toughness needed to face adversity.

- Seek Out Stoic Role Models: Reading about stoicism and learning from stoic role models can help you develop a stoic mindset. Some famous stoics include Marcus Aurelius, Epictetus, and Seneca.

THE BREAKDOWN:

Developing a stoic mindset is important when facing adversity. It allows us to regulate our emotions, build resilience, and maintain a sense of control over the situation. By focusing on what we can control, practicing mindfulness, embracing discomfort, and seeking out stoic role models, we can develop the mental toughness needed to face adversity and grind towards success. Remember, being stoic is not about suppressing emotions, but rather about regulating them and maintaining a calm and rational mindset in the face of adversity.

Remaining Stoic in the Heart of Detroit

Growing up in Detroit is an experience unlike any other. From the moment you step foot in the city, you can feel its unique energy, a blend of raw passion and resilience. Detroit demands a certain mentality, a strength of character that becomes essential for navigating the challenges that arise amidst its contrasting landscape of crime and creativity. In Lesson No. 9, we delve into the importance of remaining stoic in the face of adversity, exploring how this philosophical approach can serve as a guiding principle for survival and personal growth in the Motor City.

The Detroit Mentality:

The Detroit mentality is shaped by a history of struggle, economic downturns, and a reputation for high crime rates. The city's residents have witnessed the rise and fall of industries, the effects of urban decay, and the ever-present shadow of violence. To thrive in such an environment, one must cultivate a resilient mindset that embraces stoicism as a means of finding inner strength and stability amidst chaos.

Stoicism as a Path to Resilience:

Stoicism, an ancient philosophy founded on principles of self-control and emotional resilience, provides a framework for maintaining composure in the face of adversity. It teaches us to focus on what is within our control, to accept the imperfections of the world, and to cultivate an unwavering determination to overcome obstacles. In Detroit, where daily challenges can be overwhelming, adopting a stoic demeanor becomes crucial for survival.

The Dichotomy of Crime and Creativity:

In Detroit, crime and creativity exist side by side, creating a unique duality that both shapes and challenges its residents. The city has a rich cultural heritage, with a vibrant music scene, an influential artistic community, and a legacy of innovation. However, it also faces significant crime rates and social issues that can test even the strongest of spirits. Remaining stoic allows individuals to navigate this dichotomy, embracing creativity as an outlet for expression while maintaining a vigilant mindset to protect themselves and their communities.

Emotional Detachment and Inner Strength:

Remaining stoic in Detroit requires a delicate balance between emotional detachment and inner strength. It means learning to control our reactions to external circumstances, not allowing ourselves to be overwhelmed by fear, anger, or despair. By cultivating emotional resilience, we can find the clarity of mind necessary to make wise decisions and take purposeful action, even in the face of adversity.

Applying Stoicism to Daily Life:

In this chapter, we explore practical strategies for applying stoic principles to everyday situations in Detroit. We delve into topics such as managing fear in dangerous neighborhoods, finding meaning in challenging circumstances, fostering community resilience, and developing an unwavering sense of self amidst external pressures. Through anecdotes, examples, and philosophical teachings, we provide actionable advice for embracing stoicism as a way of life in the city.

THE BREAKDOWN:

Lesson No. 9: Remaining Stoic illuminates the importance of adopting a stoic demeanor as an essential tool for navigating the unique challenges of growing up in Detroit. By embracing the principles of stoicism, residents can develop the mental fortitude necessary to thrive in an environment that demands strength, resilience, and a relentless pursuit of personal growth. As we explore the dichotomy of crime and creativity, we discover that stoicism not only provides a path to survival but also unlocks the potential for transformation, allowing individuals to rise above their circumstances and contribute positively to the vibrant tapestry of Detroit's collective resilience.

LESSON NO. 10
LEVERAGE THE LLC OR C-CORP/S-CORP

Leveraging business:
"Game of power, amplifying gains, and dominating markets with calculated moves."

—*BUILD*

WHEN IT COMES to starting a business, one of the most important decisions you'll make is choosing the right legal structure. Two popular options for small businesses are the Limited Liability Company (LLC) and the C Corporation (C-Corp). In this chapter, we'll explore the advantages and disadvantages of each and how they can provide leverage for your business.

Limited Liability Company (LLC)

An LLC is a popular choice for small businesses because it offers the advantages of a corporation while providing flexibility and simplicity. Here are some of the benefits of starting an LLC:

- Limited Liability Protection: As the name suggests, an LLC provides limited liability protection, meaning that your personal assets are protected if your business is sued or goes bankrupt.

- Flexibility in Management: Unlike corporations, LLCs have a lot of flexibility in management structure. You can choose to have a single member or multiple members, and the members can manage the business themselves or hire outside managers.

- Pass-Through Taxation: LLCs have pass-through taxation, meaning that the business itself doesn't pay taxes on its income. Instead, the income is passed through to the members who report it on their personal tax returns.

C Corporation (C-Corp)

A C-Corp is a separate legal entity from its owners, meaning that it can own assets, incur liabilities, and pay taxes in its own name. Here are some of the advantages of starting a C-Corp:

- Limited Liability Protection: Like an LLC, a C-Corp provides limited liability protection for its owners. This means that the owners' personal assets are protected if the business is sued or goes bankrupt.

- Perpetual Existence: A C-Corp has perpetual existence, meaning that it continues to exist even if the owners die or sell their shares.

- Easier Access to Capital: C-Corps can raise capital through the sale of stocks, which makes it easier to attract investors and raise money.

Choosing the Right Legal Structure

Deciding between an LLC and a C-Corp can be a difficult decision. However, it's important to choose the right structure based on the needs of your business. Here are some things to consider:

Liability Protection: If you're concerned about personal liability, an LLC or C-Corp may be the right choice for you.

- Tax Implications: LLCs have pass-through taxation, which can be advantageous for some small businesses. However, C-Corps have more tax benefits and can offer more deductions.

- Ownership Structure: If you want more flexibility in ownership structure, an LLC may be the better choice. However, if you plan on raising capital through the sale of stocks, a C-Corp may be the better choice.

Starting a business at a young age can be challenging, but it can also be incredibly rewarding. When you start a business at a young age, you have the advantage of time on your side. You have more years to learn, grow, and develop your skills, which can lead to greater success in the long run. Additionally, starting a business at a young age can help you build your network and establish a reputation early on.

When it comes to starting an LLC or C-Corp at a young age, there are a few additional considerations to keep in mind. First, it's important to consider the legal and financial implications of starting a business. Depending on your age, you may need to involve a parent or guardian in the process, as you may not be legally allowed to sign contracts or make financial decisions on your own.

Second,

It's important to consider your long-term goals for the business.

Are you starting the business as a hobby or a side hustle, or do you plan on turning it into a full-time career? If you're starting the business as a side hustle, an LLC or sole proprietorship may be the right choice. However, if you plan on turning it into a full-time career and raising capital, a C-Corp may be the better choice.

THE'BREAKDOWN:

Starting a business at a young age can be an incredible learning experience. You'll have the opportunity to develop your skills in a real-world setting, and you'll learn valuable lessons about marketing, sales, finance, and management. Additionally, starting a business can help you develop important life skills like responsibility, accountability, and time management. Overall, starting an LLC or C-Corp at a young age can provide leverage for your future success. By taking advantage of your youth, you can build and position yourself for long-term growth and profitability. Starting an LLC or C-Corp can provide leverage for your business by offering limited liability protection, flexibility in management, and easier access to capital. Choosing the right legal structure is an important decision that should be based on the needs of your business. When deciding between an LLC and a C-Corp, consider the liability protection, tax implications, and ownership structure. With the right legal structure, you'll be able to protect your personal assets and position your business for success. With hard work, dedication, and a willingness to learn, you can turn your entrepreneurial dreams into a reality.

LESSON NO. 11
THE IMPORTANCE OF SKILLED TRADES

Skilled trades:
"The hidden gold mine, where expertise crafts fortunes, and mastery sparks wealth."

—*BUILD*

IN TODAY'S FAST-PACED world, there is a lot of emphasis on getting a college education and pursuing a white-collar career. However, skilled trades offer an often-overlooked path to success and financial stability. In this chapter, we'll explore why learning skilled trades is so important and how you can get started. I've always prided myself on my ability to learn quickly and absorb new information. I'm the kind of person who can watch a YouTube video on how to do something and then go out and do it myself. This skill has served me well in my career, which has been in the skilled trades. Started out as a sheet metal mechanic, and I quickly learned that I loved the work. I enjoyed the challenge of working with my hands and creating something new. I also liked the fact that I was always learning new things. There was always something new to learn, whether it was a new technique or a new way to use a tool.

After a few years as a sheet metal mechanic, I decided to move into quality inspection. This was a lateral move, but it was something that I was interested in. I wanted to learn more about how to ensure the quality of products, and I thought that a career in quality inspection would give me that opportunity. I'm now at the time of me writing this book a quality inspector for a large manufacturing company, and I love my job. I get to use my skills to make sure that the products that we produce are of the highest quality. I also get to work with a great team of people, and I feel like I'm making a difference in the world.

If you're thinking about a career in the skilled trades, I highly recommend it. It's a great way to use your hands, learn new things, and make a good living. There are many different types of skilled trades, so you're sure to find one that's a good fit for you. In addition to the benefits that I mentioned above, a career in the skilled trades also offers the following:

JOB SECURITY:

There is always a demand for skilled tradespeople. As our infrastructure ages, the need for skilled tradespeople will only increase.

SOLID PAY:

Skilled tradespeople earn good wages. The median annual wage for construction workers was $40,710 in 2020.

OPPORTUNITIES FOR ADVANCEMENT:

There are many opportunities for advancement in the skilled trades. With experience and training, you can move up the ranks and earn even higher wages.

LEVERAGE:

When you make 6 figures, you have a lot of financial leverage. This means that you can borrow money to invest in stocks, real estate, or other assets. This can help you to grow your wealth much faster than if you were only investing your own money.

INVESTING:

When you invest in stocks, you are buying a piece of ownership in a company. If the company does well, the value of your stocks will go up. This can be a great way to grow your wealth over time. However, it is important to remember that there is always risk involved in investing. You could lose money if the company does not do well.

UNDISTURBED 99% OF THE TIME:

It is impossible to say with 100% certainty that you will make money when you invest in stocks. However, there are a few things you can do to increase your chances of success. First, you should do your research and invest in companies that you believe have good prospects for growth. Second, you should diversify your portfolio by investing in a variety of different companies. This will help to reduce your risk if one company does not do well. Finally, you should be patient and don't panic if the market takes a downturn. The stock market is cyclical and there will be ups and downs. If you stay invested for the long term, you are more likely to see your investment grow. In your case, you were able to leverage the logistical demand of your position to freely do what you really wanted, which was stock investing while working. This is a great example of how you can use your skills and knowledge to your advantage. If you can find a job that allows you to have some free time, you can use that time to invest in stocks or other assets. This can help you to grow your wealth and achieve your financial goals.

HERE ARE SOME TIPS ON INVESTING WHILE WORKING:

- Do your research: Before you invest in any stock, make sure you do your research and understand the company. You should also consider the overall market conditions before making any investment decisions.

- Diversify your portfolio: Don't put all your eggs in one basket. By diversifying your portfolio, you can reduce your risk if one stock or sector of the market performs poorly.

- Be patient: The stock market is cyclical and there will be ups and downs. Don't panic if the market takes a downturn. If you stay invested for the long term, you are more likely to see your investment grow. If you follow these tips, you can increase your chances of success when investing in stocks while working.

Why is Learning Skilled Trades Important?

Here are a few reasons why learning skilled trades is so important:

- Job Security: Skilled trades are always in demand, and many industries are currently facing a shortage of skilled workers. By learning a trade, you can enjoy job security and a steady stream of work.

- High Wages: Skilled trades typically offer higher wages than many other types of jobs, especially for those with specialized skills and certifications.

- Hands-On Work: For those who enjoy working with their hands and seeing the results of their labor, skilled trades can offer a sense of satisfaction and fulfillment that may be lacking in other types of work.

- Entrepreneurship: Many skilled trades can be pursued as a self-employed entrepreneur, offering the opportunity to be your own boss and build your own business.

How to Learn Skilled Trades

If you're interested in learning a skilled trade, here are a few tips to help you get started:

- Explore Your Options: There are many different types of skilled trades, including carpentry, plumbing, electrical work, HVAC, and welding, among others. Research different trades to find one that interests you and aligns with your skills and strengths.

- Get Certified: Many skilled trades require certification or licensure, which can typically be obtained through a combination of education, apprenticeships, and exams. Look for programs in your area that offer training and certification in your chosen trade.

- Network: Building relationships with others in your industry can be a valuable way to learn new skills, find job opportunities, and stay up to date on industry trends.

Attend industry events and join professional organizations to connect with others in your field.

- Stay Current: Skilled trades are constantly evolving, with new technologies and techniques emerging all the time. Make a commitment to ongoing learning and professional development to stay current and advance your career.

The ROI of your aviation education can be calculated by dividing the total amount of money you earned after completing your education by the cost of your education. In your case, the total amount of money you earned after completing your education is $120,000 - $40,000 = $80,000. The cost of your education is $31,000. Therefore, your ROI is $80,000 / $31,000 = 2.58. This means that for every dollar you invested in your education, you earned $2.58 in return.

It is important to note that this is just a simple calculation and does not consider other factors, such as the cost of living, inflation, and the opportunity cost of your time. However, it does give you a general idea of the potential ROI of your aviation education. If you are considering a career in aviation, it is important to weigh the costs and benefits carefully. The cost of your education can be significant, but the potential rewards can be even greater. If you are passionate about aviation and are willing to work hard, you can earn a good living and have a rewarding career.

Here are some additional factors to consider when calculating the ROI of your aviation education:

- The cost of living: The cost of living in the area where you will be working will affect your overall expenses. If the cost of living is high, you will need to earn a higher salary to maintain your standard of living.

- Inflation: Inflation can erode the value of your earnings over time. If inflation is high, you will need to earn a higher salary to maintain your purchasing power.

- The opportunity cost of your time: The opportunity cost of your time is the amount of money you could have earned if you had worked instead of going to school. If you can earn a good salary while you are in school, the opportunity cost of your time will be lower.

THE BREAKDOWN:

Learning a skilled trade can be a powerful path to success and financial stability. By choosing a trade that interests you, obtaining the necessary certification and training, and committing to ongoing learning and professional development, you can build a successful career and enjoy the benefits of a stable, rewarding profession. So, whether you're just starting out or looking to make a career change, consider learning a skilled trade and take the first step towards grinding towards success.

LESSON NO. 12
THE IMPORTANCE OF GOOD CREDIT

Good credit:
"The key to kingdoms, unlocking opportunities, and commanding financial dominion."

—BUILD

WHEN IT COMES to achieving financial stability and success, few things are as important as having good credit. Your credit score is a measure of your financial responsibility, and it can impact your ability to obtain loans, credit cards, mortgages, and even employment opportunities. In this chapter, we'll explore why having good credit is so important, and how you can take steps to improve your credit score.

Why is Good Credit Important?

There are many reasons why having good credit is important. Here are just a few:

Access to Loans:

If you ever need to borrow money for a major purchase, such as a home or car, your credit score will be one of the main factors that lenders consider when deciding whether to approve your loan application. A good credit score can help you qualify for lower interest rates and better loan terms, which can save you thousands of dollars in the long run.

Credit Cards:

Credit cards can be a valuable financial tool, allowing you to make purchases and earn rewards points or cash back. However, if you have poor credit, you may have a harder time getting approved for a credit card, and you may be subject to higher interest rates and fees.

Employment Opportunities:

Some employers may run credit checks as part of the hiring process, particularly for jobs that involve financial responsibility or require security clearance. A poor credit score could potentially hurt your chances of getting hired for these types of jobs.

Renting a Home or Apartment:

Many landlords and property managers run credit checks on potential tenants. If you have a low credit score, you may have a harder time renting a home or apartment, or you may be required to pay a higher security deposit.

How to Improve Your Credit Score

If your credit score isn't where you want it to be, don't worry.

There are steps you can take to improve it. Here are a few tips:

Pay Your Bills on Time:

Payment history is one of the most important factors that determine your credit score. Make sure you pay all your bills on time, every time. Consider setting up automatic payments or reminders to help you stay on track.

Reduce Your Debt:

The amount of debt you have compared to your credit limit, also known as your credit utilization ratio, is another important factor that impacts your credit score. Try to keep your credit card balances low and pay off your debts as quickly as possible.

Check Your Credit Report:

You are entitled to a free credit report from each of the three major credit bureaus (Equifax, Experian, and TransUnion) once a year. Check your report regularly to make sure there are no errors or fraudulent activity.

Don't Apply for Too Much Credit:

Every time you apply for credit, it can have a temporary negative impact on your credit score. Be selective about the credit you apply for, and only apply for what you need.

The importance of building Business Credit:

Access to capital:

Having good business credit can help you to access capital, which you can use to grow your business. You can use capital to purchase inventory, hire employees, or expand your operations.

Improved terms:

When you have good business credit, you can often get better terms on loans and lines of credit. This means that you may be able to get a lower interest rate or a longer repayment period.

Increased credibility:

Having good business credit can help you to build credibility with suppliers and customers. This can make it easier to get the goods and services you need for your business.

Reduced risk:

When you have good business credit, you are less likely to default on loans or lines of credit. This can help to protect your business from financial hardship.

Here are some examples of what specifically business credit can do for the small business owner:

Purchase inventory:

If you have a retail business, you need to purchase inventory in order to sell products to your customers. Having good business credit can help you to get a loan or line of credit to purchase inventory.

Hire employees:

If you need to hire employees, you will need to pay them a salary or wage. Having good business credit can help you to get a loan or line of credit to cover the cost of payroll.

Expand your operations:

If you want to expand your business, you will need to invest in new equipment, facilities, or marketing. Having good business credit can help you to get a loan or line of credit to cover the cost of expansion.

If you are a small business owner, building business credit is an asset. It can help you to access capital, improve your terms, increase your credibility, and reduce your risk.

There are several ways to build business credit, including:

Open a business credit card:

A business credit card is a great way to start building business credit. Use the card for business expenses and pay the bill in full each month.

Get a business loan:

A business loan can help you to access capital for your business. Make sure to shop around and compare interest rates before you choose a lender.

Use a business line of credit:

A business line of credit is a revolving line of credit that you can use as needed. This can be a good option if you need to access capital on an occasional basis.

Building business credit takes time and effort, but it is worth it. By following these tips, you can start building business credit and improve your chances of success.

THE BREAKDOWN:

Having good credit is essential for achieving financial success and stability. By understanding why good credit is important and taking steps to improve your credit score, you can open new opportunities and avoid unnecessary financial stress. Make building good credit a priority, and you'll be on your way to grinding towards financial freedom.

LESSON NO. 13
IMPORTANCE OF LEARNING STOCK INVESTING

WHEN IT COMES to building wealth and achieving financial success, few things are as powerful as investing in the stock market. However, many people are intimidated by the world of investing and believe that it is something only the wealthy can do. In this chapter, we'll explore why learning stock investing is so important, and how you can take steps to become a savvy investor. According to the Federal Reserve, the percentage of Americans with a net worth of $2.3 million or more was 0.7% in 2023. This means that only about 7 out of every 1,000 Americans had a net worth of $2.3 million or more. Ironically, at the time of writing this book, 2.3 million is my current net worth via trading/investing into the stock market.

The distribution of wealth in the United States is highly unequal. The top 1% of Americans own more than 38% of the country's wealth. The bottom 50% of Americans own less than 1% of the country's wealth. There are several factors that contribute to this inequality. One factor is that the wealthy tend to earn more money than the poor. They also tend to have more assets, such as stocks, bonds, and real estate. This allows them to accumulate wealth over time. Another factor that contributes to inequality is that the wealthy have access to better education and healthcare than the poor. This gives them an advantage in the labor market and allows them to earn more money. The government can take steps to reduce inequality, such as by increasing taxes on the wealthy and providing more assistance to the poor. However, it is difficult to address inequality without addressing the underlying causes, such as discrimination and lack of opportunity.

Income from trading and investing is "ordinary income" and is taxed at the same rates as their salary would be. The author's tax bracket will depend on their filing status and their total income. For example, if the author is single and has a taxable income of $2.3 million, they would be in the top tax bracket, which is currently 37%.

Here is a breakdown of the federal income tax brackets for 2023:

10%: For taxable income of $0 to $41,775

12%: For taxable income of $41,776 to $89,075

22%: For taxable income of $89,076 to $167,540

24%: For taxable income of $167,541 to $208,896

32%: For taxable income of $208,897 to $523,600

35%: For taxable income of $523,601 to $1,046,800

37%: For taxable income of $1,046,801 or more

Here is a breakdown of how the compounding effect works when it comes to dividend stocks and index funds:

Dividend stocks are stocks that pay out a portion of their earnings to shareholders in the form of dividends. Index funds are a type of mutual fund that tracks a specific market index, such as the S&P 500. The compounding effect is the ability of your investments to grow over time due to the reinvestment of dividends and capital gains. When you reinvest your dividends and capital gains, you are essentially buying more shares of stock. This means that your investment will grow at a faster rate than if you simply held onto your shares and did not reinvest anything.

For example, let's say you invest $10,000 in a dividend stock that pays out a 5% dividend yield. This means that you will receive $500 in dividends each year. If you reinvest these dividends, you will have $10,500 in your account after one year. The next year, you will receive $525 in dividends, which you can reinvest. This process will continue year after year, and your investment will grow at a faster and faster rate.

The same principle applies to index funds. When you invest in an index fund, you are essentially buying a small piece of every company in the index. This means that you are diversified, and your investment is less likely to be affected by the performance of any one company. Index funds are a good option for investors who want to grow their wealth over time. They are low-cost and easy to invest in. If you are new to investing, index funds are a good place to start.

Here are some tips for maximizing the compounding effect:

Invest for the long term: The longer you invest, the more time your money must grow.

Reinvest your dividends and capital gains:

This will help your investment grow at a faster rate.

Diversify your portfolio:

This will help reduce your risk.

Invest in low-cost index funds:

Index funds are a good way to diversify your portfolio and keep your costs low.

There are a few factors that contribute to this inequality. One factor is that the wealthy tend to earn more money than the poor. They also tend to have more assets, such as stocks, bonds, and real estate. This allows them to accumulate wealth over time.

Why is Learning Stock Investing Important?

Here are a few reasons why learning stock investing is so important:

Building Wealth:

The stock market has historically been one of the best ways to build wealth over the long term. By investing in stocks, you can benefit from the growth of some of the world's most successful companies.

Beating Inflation:

Inflation is the steady rise in the cost of goods and services over time. Investing in stocks can help you keep pace with inflation and ensure that your money retains its value over time.

Retirement Planning:

Investing in the stock market can be a powerful tool for building a retirement nest egg. By starting early and consistently investing over time, you can benefit from the power of compound interest and potentially build a sizable retirement fund.

Diversification:

Investing in stocks allows you to diversify your portfolio and spread your risk across a range of different companies and industries.

How to Learn Stock Investing

If you're new to investing, the thought of getting started can be overwhelming. Here are a few tips to help you get started:

Educate Yourself:

Take the time to learn the basics of investing, including key concepts such as risk, diversification, and asset allocation. There are plenty of online resources, books, and courses available to help you get started.

Start Small:

When you're first starting out, it's important to start small and avoid taking on too much risk. Consider investing in a low-cost index fund or exchange-traded fund (ETF) that tracks the overall stock market.

Be Patient:

Investing in the stock market requires patience and a

long-term perspective. Avoid making emotional decisions based on short-term market fluctuations and focus on your long-term goals.

Seek Professional Help:

If you're feeling overwhelmed or unsure about investing, consider seeking help from a financial advisor or investment professional. They can provide valuable guidance and help you build a personalized investment strategy that aligns with your goals.

THE BREAKDOWN:

Learning stock investing is an important step towards achieving financial success and building long-term wealth. By understanding the benefits of investing in the stock market and taking steps to educate yourself, you can start building a portfolio that aligns with your goals and helps you achieve financial freedom. Make investing a priority, and you'll be well on your way to grinding towards financial success.

LESSON NO. 14
TAPPING INTO YOUR BIRTHRIGHT
(HIDDEN POTIENTIAL)

Potential:
"The untamed beast within, waiting to be
unleashed, propelling you towards limitless success."

—BUILD

ONE OF THE harshest truths in life is that many people fail to fulfill their full potential. Despite having the ability to achieve great things, they fall short due to a lack of effort, focus, or perseverance. This can lead to feelings of regret and unfulfillment later in life. There are several reasons why people fail to fulfill their full potential. One of the main reasons is fear. Fear of failure, fear of success, fear of the unknown - all of these can hold people back from reaching their full potential. When we let fear control our actions, we limit ourselves and miss out on opportunities for growth and success.

Another reason is a lack of discipline. Many people have

big dreams and goals, but they lack the discipline to take the necessary steps to achieve them. They may procrastinate, get distracted easily, or give up too quickly when faced with obstacles. Without discipline, it's difficult to achieve anything significant. In addition, many people don't fully understand their own potential. They may underestimate their abilities or fail to recognize their strengths. When we don't know what we're capable of, we're less likely to push ourselves to reach our full potential.

The harsh truth is that failing to fulfill your full potential can lead to a life of mediocrity and regret. You may look back on your life and wonder what could have been if you had put in more effort, taken more risks, or believed in yourself more. However, it's never too late to start fulfilling your potential. It requires self-reflection, self-discipline, and a willingness to face your fears and push past them. It also requires setting clear goals and taking consistent action towards achieving them.

Fulfilling their potential

Stephen Hawking: Stephen Hawking was born with amyotrophic lateral sclerosis (ALS), a degenerative disease that affects the nervous system. Despite his diagnosis, Hawking went on to become one of the most renowned physicists of our time. He authored several groundbreaking books, including "A Brief History of Time," and made significant contributions to our understanding of the universe.

Marie Curie: Marie Curie was a Polish physicist and chemist who conducted pioneering research on radioactivity. She was the first woman to win a Nobel Prize, and the only person to win the Nobel Prize twice. Her work has had a profound impact on our understanding of the universe and has led to the development of many life-saving medical treatments.

Nelson Mandela: Nelson Mandela was a South African

anti-apartheid revolutionary, political leader, and philanthropist who served as President of South Africa from 1994 to 1999. He was the country's first black head of state and the first elected in a fully representative democratic election. His leadership helped to end apartheid and establish a new democratic South Africa.

Not fulfilling their potential

Vincent van Gogh: Vincent van Gogh was a Dutch Post-Impressionist painter who is among the most famous and influential figures in the history of Western art. However, he struggled with mental illness and poverty throughout his life, and only sold one painting during his lifetime.

Jimi Hendrix: Jimi Hendrix was an American rock guitarist, singer, and songwriter who is widely regarded as one of the most influential musicians of all time. However, he died of a drug overdose at the age of 27, before he could fully realize his potential.

Kurt Cobain: Kurt Cobain was an American singer, songwriter, and guitarist who was the front man of the rock band Nirvana. He is considered one of the most influential musicians of the 1990s. However, he struggled with depression and addiction, and committed suicide at the age of 27.

(Author note): It is important to note that these are just a few examples, and there are many other people who have fulfilled their potential or not fulfilled their potential. Ultimately, it is up to everyone to decide how they want to live their life and what they want to achieve.

THE BREAKDOWN:

Not fulfilling one's full potential is a harsh truth that many people face. However, by acknowledging your fears, developing discipline, recognizing your strengths, and acting towards your goals, you can overcome these barriers and achieve the success and fulfillment you deserve.

LESSON NO. 15
OUTWORK YESTERDAY

Effective hard work:
"The secret weapon, combining hustle and strategy,
carving a path to triumph."

—*BUILD*

Growing up, I was fortunate to have two parents who instilled in me the importance of hard work and efficiency. My mother was a single mother who worked two jobs to support my brother and me. She never complained about her workload, and she always showed up to work on time and did her best. My father was a self-made man who started his own business from scratch. He worked long hours, but he was always willing to help around the house. Seeing my parents work hard and sacrifice so much for me taught me the value of hard work and efficiency. I decided that I wanted to be like them, and I wanted to achieve my goals through hard work and determination.

In 2023, there are more opportunities than ever to be

successful. With the help of technology, you can start a business, learn a new skill, or even become a world-class chef. However, it's important to remember that success doesn't happen overnight. It takes hard work, dedication, and perseverance.

If you're willing to put in the work, you can achieve anything you set your mind to. Don't let the victim mentality hold you back. Don't make excuses. Just get out there and start working hard.

Tips for being sharp and efficient:

Set clear goals and deadlines. When you know what you want to achieve and when you want to achieve it, you're more likely to stay on track.

Break down large tasks into smaller, more manageable ones. This will make them seem less daunting and more achievable.

Eliminate distractions. When you're working on a task, try to eliminate as many distractions as possible. This means turning off your phone, closing your email, and finding a quiet place to work.

Take breaks when you need them. Don't try to work for hours on end without taking a break. Get up and move around, or step outside for some fresh air.

Celebrate your successes. When you achieve a goal, take some time to celebrate your success. This will help you stay motivated and keep moving forward.

By following these tips, you can develop the work ethic and efficiency you need to achieve your goals.

Historical Examples:

Thomas Edison:

Edison was a self-taught inventor who is credited with over 1,000 inventions, including the light bulb, the phonograph, and the motion picture camera. He was known for his work ethic and his willingness to work long hours.

Henry Ford:

Ford was the founder of the Ford Motor Company and is credited with the development of the assembly line, which revolutionized the manufacturing industry. He was also known for his work ethic and his commitment to efficiency.

Walt Disney:

Disney was the founder of the Walt Disney Company and is credited with the creation of Mickey Mouse, Snow White and the Seven Dwarfs, and Disneyland. He was known for his creativity and his vision.

Recent Examples:

Mark Zuckerberg:

Zuckerberg is the co-founder and CEO of Facebook. He is known for his work ethic and his ability to connect people from all over the world.

Jeff Bezos:

Bezos is the founder and CEO of Amazon. He is known for his work ethic and his commitment to innovation.

Elon Musk:

Musk is the founder and CEO of Tesla and SpaceX. He is known for his work ethic and his vision for the future.

(Author Note): A study by the Harvard Business Review found that self-starters are 12 times more likely to be promoted than those who are not. The study also found that self-starters are more likely to be successful in their careers.

Here are some tips for outworking yesterday:

- Set clear goals and deadlines.

- Break down large tasks into smaller, more manageable ones.

- Eliminate distractions.

- Take breaks when you need them, but don't let them derail your progress.

- Celebrate your successes.

THE BREAKDOWN:

The ability to outwork yesterday is a key skill for anyone who wants to be successful in life. If you are willing to put in the time and effort, you can achieve anything you set your mind to.

LESSON NO. 16
RESET THE GAME

Self-resetting:
"Recalibrating, adapting, and bouncing back
stronger to conquer any challenge."

—*BUILD*

IN TODAY'S WORLD, it can be difficult to unplug from the system. We are constantly bombarded with information from our phones, computers, and TVs. This constant influx of information can be overwhelming and can lead to stress, anxiety, and burnout. If you are feeling overwhelmed by the constant barrage of information, it is important to unplug from the system from time to time. This means taking a break from technology and social media. It also means spending time in nature, reading a book, or simply doing nothing at all.

Unplugging from the system can help you to:

- Reduce stress and anxiety: When you are constantly bombarded with information, your body goes into a state of fight-or-flight. This can lead to increased levels of stress and anxiety. Unplugging from the system can help your body to relax and return to a state of balance.

- Improve your focus and concentration: When you are constantly switching between tasks, it can be difficult to focus on any one thing. Unplugging from the system can help you to focus on the task at hand and improve your productivity.

- Increase your creativity: When you are not constantly bombarded with information, you are more likely to be creative. This is because you have the time and space to think freely.

- Improve your sleep: When you are constantly using technology before bed, it can be difficult to fall asleep. Unplugging from the system before bed can help you to fall asleep more easily and get a better night's sleep.

If you are feeling overwhelmed by the constant barrage of information, it is important to unplug from the system from time to time. This can help you to reduce stress, improve your focus, increase your creativity, and improve your sleep.

Here are some tips for unplugging from the system:

- Turn off your phone: This is the most important step. When you are not constantly checking your phone, you will be less likely to be distracted.

- Delete social media apps from your phone: If you find that you are spending too much time on social media, delete the apps from your phone. This will make it more difficult to check them.

- Set limits on your screen time: Decide how much time you want to spend on technology each day and stick to it.

- Find other activities to do: When you are not using technology, find other activities to do. This could include reading, going for a walk, or spending time with friends and family.

Here are some scientific studies that have monitored the toll social media takes on the human brain:

A 2018 study published in the journal Nature found that heavy social media users had reduced gray matter density in the hippocampus, a region of the brain that is important for memory and learning.

A 2019 study published in the journal Addiction found that social media use was associated with increased levels of anxiety and depression.

A 2020 study published in the journal PLOS One found that social media use was associated with decreased levels of self-esteem.

A 2021 study published in the journal JAMA Psychiatry found that social media use was associated with an increased risk of suicide.

These studies suggest that social media use can have a negative impact on the human brain. However, it is important to note that these studies are correlational, which means that they cannot prove that social media use causes these negative effects. It is possible that people who are already anxious, depressed, or have low self-esteem are more likely to use social media.

More research is needed to determine the exact effects of social media on the brain. However, the available evidence suggests that it is important to be mindful of our social media use and to take breaks from time to time.

THE BREAKDOWN:

Unplugging from the system can be difficult, but it is worth it. When you unplug, you give your mind and body a chance to rest and recharge. This can help you to be more productive, creative, and focused.

LESSON NO. 17
THE POWER OF INDIFFERENCE

Power of indifference:
"A shield of focus, blocking distractions, and
propelling you towards unwavering success."

—BUILD

IN TODAY'S WORLD, it can be difficult to be indifferent. We are constantly bombarded with information and stimuli, and it can be hard to tune it all out. However, indifference can be a powerful tool. When used correctly, it can help us to focus on what is important, avoid wasting time and energy on things that are not, and protect our mental and emotional health.

What is Indifference?

Indifference is the state of not caring about something. It is the opposite of interest, passion, or concern. When we are indifferent to something, we do not take it personally, and we do not let it affect us emotionally.

Benefits of Indifference

There are many benefits to indifference. When we are indifferent to things that are not important to us, we can save time and energy. We can also avoid getting stressed out or upset about things that are out of our control. Indifference can also help us to focus on the things that are truly important to us.

How to Develop Indifference

Developing indifference takes practice. The first step is to identify the things that are not important to you. Once you have identified these things, you can start to train yourself to not care about them. This may be difficult at first, but it will get easier with time. There are a few things you can do to help you develop indifference. First, you can try to distance yourself from the things that are not important to you. This means avoiding them as much as possible. You can also try to change your perspective on these things. Instead of seeing them as important, try to see them as unimportant or even trivial.

Meaning

Indifference is the state of not caring about something. It is the opposite of interest, passion, or concern. When we are indifferent to something, we do not take it personally, and we do not let it affect us emotionally. There are both pros and cons to indifference.

Pros of Indifference

It can help us to stay focused on our goals. When we are indifferent to the opinions of others, we are less likely to let their criticism or praise affect our decisions. This can be especially helpful when we are trying to achieve something difficult, as we will likely face a lot of criticism from people who are not familiar with our goals.

It can help us to avoid getting stressed out. When we are indifferent to things that are out of our control, we are less likely to get stressed out about them. This can help us to maintain our mental and emotional health.

It can help us to be more productive. When we are not distracted by things that are not important to us, we can focus on the things that are truly important and get more done.

Cons of Indifference

It can lead to apathy. When we are indifferent to everything, we may become apathetic, which means that we do not care about anything. This can lead to a lack of motivation and a feeling of emptiness.

It can make it difficult to connect with others. When we are indifferent to the feelings and needs of others, it can be difficult to build relationships. This can lead to loneliness and isolation.

It can prevent us from acting. When we are indifferent to problems, we may be less likely to take action to solve them. This can lead to a worsening of the problem and a feeling of helplessness. Ultimately, whether indifference is a positive or negative thing depends on how it is used. If we can use indifference.

Historical Evidence of the Power of Indifference

There is historical evidence to suggest that indifference can be a powerful tool. For example, during the American Civil War, General Robert E. Lee was known for his indifference to pain and suffering. He was able to remain calm and focused even on the midst of battle. This indifference helped him to lead his troops to victory. Another example of the power of indifference is the story of Mahatma Gandhi. Gandhi was a leader of the Indian independence movement. He was able to achieve his goals through non-violence and civil disobedience. Gandhi's indifference to violence and hatred helped him to unite the Indian people and achieve independence for India.

THE BREAKDOWN:

Indifference is a powerful tool that can be used to improve our lives. When used correctly, it can help us to focus on what is important, avoid wasting time and energy on things that are not, and protect our mental and emotional health. If you are struggling to develop indifference, there are a few things you can do to help yourself. First, identify the things that are not important to you. Once you have identified these things, you can start to train yourself to not care about them. This may be difficult at first, but it will get easier with time. You can also try to distance yourself from the things that are not important to you. This means avoiding them as much as possible. You can also try to change your perspective on these things. Instead of seeing them as important, try to see them as unimportant or even trivial.

LESSON NO. 18
COSTLY HABITS & BAD INVESTMENTS

Cost of bad habits:
"The silent assassin, eroding fortunes, and derailing
dreams without remorse."

—BUILD

IN LESSON NO. 18, titled "Costly Habits & Bad Investments," we delve into the importance of identifying and eliminating detrimental habits and investments that hinder personal growth and financial well-being. By recognizing and redirecting our focus towards more beneficial endeavors, we can save substantial amounts of capital and allocate those resources towards self-improvement. This chapter explores various areas of life where costly habits and bad investments commonly occur and provides a system for removing them from our lives.

Identifying Poisonous Habits:

The term "poison" is used metaphorically to represent any element that subtracts from our journey or obstructs our progress. These poisonous habits can manifest in different areas of life, such as nutrition, sexuality, substance abuse, impulsive spending, and poor financial management. Let's examine some examples of these costly habits:

- Junk Food: Unhealthy eating habits not only impact our physical well-being but also drain our financial resources. Constantly indulging in fast food or processed snacks can lead to medical issues, which can be expensive to treat in the long run.

- Sexual Addiction: Engaging in excessive pornography consumption or masturbation can have negative consequences on mental health, relationships, and overall productivity. These behaviors can become addictive and consume valuable time and energy.

- Alcohol Abuse: Misusing alcohol not only poses health risks but also incurs financial costs. Frequent alcohol consumption can strain personal relationships, hinder professional growth, and lead to significant expenses.

- Chasing Immediate Pleasure: Prioritizing short-term pleasures, such as seeking sexual encounters or indulging in lavish experiences, without considering long-term financial stability can result in missed opportunities for personal growth and financial security.

- Neglecting Capital: Ignoring financial management, such as overspending, subscribing to unnecessary streaming applications, or failing to track expenses, can deplete our capital without us realizing it. These habits prevent us from making meaningful investments in ourselves.

- Rabbit Hole Spending: Abusing credit and accumulating debt by overspending or purchasing unnecessary items can have severe consequences. High-interest rates and mounting debt can limit our financial freedom and impede our ability to invest in more valuable assets.

Creating a System for Elimination:

To free up resources for self-investment and personal growth, it is essential to develop a system that helps identify and eliminate these costly habits. Here is a suggested framework for implementing positive changes:

- Awareness and Reflection: Begin by acknowledging the harmful habits that exist in your life. Reflect on how these habits are impacting your overall well-being, finances, and personal growth. Understanding the negative consequences is crucial for motivation.

- Prioritization: Identify your larger passions and long-term goals. Determine the activities and investments that align with these aspirations and provide genuine value to your life.

- Accountability: Enlist the support of trusted friends, mentors, or support groups to hold you accountable for your progress. Regular check-ins and open discussions about your journey can help reinforce positive changes.

- Continuous Improvement: Be patient with yourself during the process of eliminating these habits. It takes time to break ingrained patterns. Embrace a growth mindset and focus on continuous improvement rather than expecting immediate perfection.

THE BREAKDOWN:

Lesson No. 18 highlights the importance of recognizing and eliminating costly habits and bad investments. By identifying poisonous vices and redirecting our focus towards more beneficial endeavors, we can save valuable financial resources and invest them in self-improvement. Through increased awareness, prioritization, and accountability, we can replace detrimental habits with healthier alternatives that align with our long-term goals.

LESSON NO. 19
LEVERAGE YOUR METHODS –
UNLEASHING YOUR NATURAL TALENTS

Unique talents:
The golden edge, carving your niche, dominating
markets, and leaving rivals in awe."

—*BUILD*

WELCOME TO LESSON No. 19, where we delve into the core principles of self-governance and embracing our unique modus operandi. In this chapter, we will explore the importance of identifying and leveraging our natural talents and abilities. Regardless of your background or work ethic, understanding and utilizing your inherent strengths can be the key to achieving extraordinary success in the world of finance and beyond.

Discovering Your Natural Gifts:

Each one of us possesses a set of innate talents and abilities that differentiate us from others. These gifts, when recognized and harnessed, can serve as powerful tools for achieving greatness. Here's how you can uncover your natural gifts:

- Introspection: Take time to reflect on your life experiences and the activities that have brought you joy and fulfillment. Identify the tasks or skills that come naturally to you, where you excel effortlessly.

- Feedback and Observations: Seek feedback from others who know you well, such as mentors, friends, or colleagues. Their perspectives can provide valuable insights into your strengths and talents. Pay attention to patterns and recurring compliments or acknowledgments.

- Passion and Excitement: Notice the activities that ignite your passion and enthusiasm. What subjects or tasks do you find yourself gravitating towards with an insatiable curiosity? Your natural talents often align with your genuine interests.

- Trial and Error: Be open to experimentation and trying new things. Don't be afraid to explore different areas to identify what resonates with you. Sometimes, it takes stepping outside of your comfort zone to discover hidden talents.

Leveraging Your Natural Talents:

Once you have identified your natural gifts, it's crucial to leverage them strategically. Here's how you can maximize the impact of your talents in the world of finance:

- Specialization: Focus on honing your skills and becoming

an expert in your chosen field. By specializing, you position yourself as an asset with unique insights and abilities.

- Collaborative Advantage: Surround yourself with a diverse network of individuals who complement your strengths. Form strategic alliances and partnerships that allow you to leverage each other's talents for mutual growth and success.

- Delegate and Outsource: Recognize areas where your talents are not as strong and delegate or outsource those tasks to individuals who excel in those areas. This frees up your time and energy to focus on activities where you can deliver exceptional results.

- Continuous Learning: Invest in ongoing education and professional development to further enhance your natural talents. Stay up to date with industry trends, advancements, and best practices to remain at the cutting edge of your field.

- Self-Awareness and Self-Governance: Understand your limitations and weaknesses, as well as your strengths. Be honest with yourself and delegate tasks that don't align with your talents. Embrace self-governance by designing your workflow and decision-making processes around your unique abilities.

THE BREAKDOWN:

In Lesson No. 19, we've explored the critical importance of leveraging your natural talents and abilities to achieve remarkable success. By identifying your inherent gifts through introspection, feedback, passion, and experimentation, you can align your efforts with what truly sets you apart. By focusing on specialization, collaboration, delegation, continuous learning, and practicing self-governance, you can maximize the impact of your talents in the finance world and beyond. Embrace your modus operandi and unleash your full potential in the pursuit of financial greatness. Remember, your unique talents are your competitive advantage in the marketplace, so leverage them wisely and watch your success soar.

LESSON NO. 20
MENTORSHIP FOR HIRE – UNLOCKING THE POWER OF GUIDANCE

Mentorship's might:
"Secret weapon, unlocking wisdom, forging connections, and accelerating the journey."

—*BUILD*

IN LESSON NO. 20, we delve into the concept of leverage once again, exploring how individuals often choose the path of servitude instead of embracing personal freedom. This chapter discusses the availability of mentorship in the modern era, emphasizing that in the year 2023 (AT THE TIME OF ME WRITING THIS), the excuse of not being able to find a mentor in your desired field no longer holds weight. We will explore online resources and platforms where mentorship can be obtained in exchange for compensation, highlighting the value of investing in guidance and knowledge.

The Power of Mentorship:

Mentorship plays a crucial role in personal and professional development. Having a mentor who possesses expertise and experience in your desired field can provide valuable insights, guidance, and support on your journey to success. However, many individuals mistakenly believe that finding a mentor is an arduous task or that they are simply inaccessible. In the digital age, this notion is no longer valid.

Online Resources for Mentorship:

Skill share:

Skill share is a popular online learning platform that offers a wide range of courses taught by industry professionals. Through Skill share, you can access mentorship-style guidance from experts in various fields. By enrolling in relevant courses, you can learn from experienced professionals and receive personalized feedback on your progress.

Udemy:

Udemy is another well-known e-learning platform that provides access to a vast library of courses across multiple disciplines. Many instructors on Udemy offer mentorship options, allowing you to engage with them directly, seek guidance, and receive personalized advice.

Clarity.fm:

Clarity.fm is a platform that connects entrepreneurs and professionals with mentors who offer their expertise on a per-minute consulting basis. Here, you can find mentors in various industries who can provide valuable insights, advice, and direction for a fee.

LinkedIn Learning:

LinkedIn Learning, formerly known as Lynda.com, is an e-learning platform that offers a vast library of courses taught by industry experts. While not explicitly focused on mentorship, LinkedIn Learning provides an opportunity to learn from seasoned professionals and gain insights from their expertise.

Masterclass:

Masterclass is an online platform that offers classes taught by renowned experts in their respective fields. By enrolling in a Masterclass, you gain access to exclusive mentorship-style guidance from icons in various industries, providing unique insights and perspectives.

Investing in Mentorship:

While mentorship for hire may require financial investment, it is important to view it as an investment in yourself and your future. The knowledge, guidance, and support gained from experienced professionals can accelerate your progress and help you avoid costly mistakes. Consider the following benefits of investing in mentorship:

Shortened Learning Curve:

A mentor can share their knowledge and experiences, helping you navigate challenges more efficiently and avoid common pitfalls.

Expanded Network:

Through mentorship, you can tap into your mentor's network, gaining access to valuable connections and opportunities.

Personalized Guidance:

A mentor provides personalized guidance tailored to your specific needs and goals, offering insights and advice that are directly applicable to your journey.

Accountability and Support:

A mentor can hold you accountable, provide encouragement, and support you during challenging times, increasing your chances of success.

THE BREAKDOWN:

In Lesson No. 20, we emphasize that finding a mentor in your desired field is no longer an excuse in the year 2023. Online resources and platforms have made mentorship accessible and available for those willing to invest in their growth. By utilizing platforms such as Skill share, Udemy, Clarity.fm, LinkedIn Learning, and Masterclass, you can tap into the knowledge and guidance of experienced professionals. Remember, mentorship is a valuable investment in your personal and professional Accountability and Support: A mentor can hold you accountable, provide encouragement, and support you during challenging times, increasing your chances of success.

Historical Examples of the Power of Mentoring:

Throughout history, the power and leverage that arise from proper mentoring have been demonstrated time and again. Let's explore some notable examples that highlight the profound impact of mentorship:

Warren Buffett and Benjamin Graham:

Warren Buffett, one of the most successful investors of our

time, attributes a significant part of his success to his mentor, Benjamin Graham. Graham, an economist and investor, imparted his wisdom and value investing principles to Buffett, shaping his investment philosophy and approach. Buffett's journey from a humble investor to a billionaire can be attributed, in part, to the guidance and mentorship he received from Graham.

Steve Jobs and Mike Markkula:

Steve Jobs, the visionary behind Apple Inc., had a critical mentor in Mike Markkula, an early investor and executive at Apple. Markkula not only provided financial support but also guided Jobs in strategic decision-making and helped shape the culture of the company. Markkula's mentorship played a pivotal role in Apple's early success and the creation of iconic products that revolutionized the tech industry.

Maya Angelou and Langston Hughes:

Maya Angelou, the celebrated poet and civil rights activist, found mentorship in renowned poet Langston Hughes. Hughes encouraged Angelou's writing, nurtured her talents, and provided guidance during her formative years as a writer. The mentorship relationship between Angelou and Hughes propelled Angelou's career, leading her to become one of the most influential voices in literature.

Negative Comparison - The Absence of Mentoring:

While the power of proper mentoring is evident, the absence of mentoring can have detrimental consequences. Let's explore a negative comparison to even out the content:

Nick Leeson and Barings Bank:

Nick Leeson's story serves as a cautionary tale of the absence of effective mentoring. Leeson, a trader at Barings Bank in the 1990s, engaged in unauthorized trading activities, leading to massive losses and ultimately causing the bank's collapse. Leeson lacked proper guidance and mentorship, which could have potentially prevented the catastrophic outcome. His story underscores the importance of mentorship in shaping ethical decision-making and risk management.

Richard Fuld and Lehman Brothers:

Richard Fuld, the former CEO of Lehman Brothers, presided over the firm during its infamous collapse in 2008, triggering a global financial crisis. Fuld's leadership and decision-making came under scrutiny, as the absence of effective mentorship and oversight allowed risky practices to prevail within the organization. The downfall of Lehman Brothers highlights the destructive consequences that can arise when leadership lacks the guidance and mentorship necessary to navigate complex financial landscapes.

THE BREAKDOWN:

Looking back at historical examples, proper mentoring has the power to shape and elevate individuals and organizations. Mentors provide invaluable guidance, knowledge, and support, propelling their mentees toward success. From Warren Buffett and Benjamin Graham's partnership to Steve Jobs and Mike Markkula's collaboration, mentorship has proven to be a driving force behind remarkable achievements. Conversely, the absence of mentorship, as seen in the cases of Nick Leeson and Richard Fuld, serves as a stark reminder of the potential pitfalls and devastating consequences that can arise without proper guidance. To maximize our potential and mitigate risks, we must embrace the power of mentorship and actively seek out mentors who can provide invaluable insights and help us navigate the complexities of the financial world.

LESSON NO. 21
PROTECT THE BAG, AT ALL COST.

Protecting capital:
"Fortress of wealth, guarding against risk, preserving gains, and ensuring dominion."

—*BUILD*

IN THIS LESSON, we will discuss the importance of protecting your wealth from unnecessary taxation. We will explore several strategies for doing so, including leveraging whole life insurance as a borrowing device. I've been in the game for a long time. I've seen it all, from the good to the bad to the ugly. And I've learned a thing or two along the way. One of the most important things I've learned is to protect the bag. The bag is your money, your assets, your livelihood. It's everything you've worked for. And it's something you need to protect at all costs.

There are a lot of ways to protect the bag. You can invest in safe assets, like real estate or whole life insurance. You can diversify your portfolio, so you're not putting all your eggs in one basket. And you can make sure you have a solid financial plan in place.

But one of the most important things you can do to protect the bag is to learn about tax havens. Tax havens are countries or jurisdictions that have very low taxes. This means that you can move your money to a tax haven and save a lot of money on taxes. I learned about tax havens a few years ago. I was reading an article about how wealthy people were using tax havens to avoid paying taxes. I was intrigued, so I did some more research. Learned that there are a lot of different tax havens out there. Some of the most popular tax havens include Switzerland, the Cayman Islands, and the Bahamas. Learned that there are a lot of different ways to use tax havens. You can move your money to a tax haven and invest it there. You can set up a corporation in a tax haven and use it to hold your assets. Or you can even buy a whole life insurance policy in a tax haven.

I decided to use whole life insurance to protect my bag. I bought a whole life insurance policy in a tax haven and invested the money in the policy. This allowed me to save a lot of money on taxes and protect my assets from creditors. Glad I learned about tax havens. They've helped me protect my bag and save a lot of money. If you're looking for ways to protect your bag, I encourage you to learn about tax havens.

How I gradually learned about tax havens and how I leveraged them to acquire multi-family property tax-free:

Started out by reading articles and doing research online. Learned about the different types of tax havens and how they worked and learned about the different ways to use tax havens to protect your assets and save money on taxes. (The internet is your friend) Once I had a good understanding of tax havens, I started to think about how to use them to acquire multi-family property. Realized that you could buy a whole life insurance policy in a tax haven and invest the money in the policy. One prime benefit of this is it would allow an individual to save a lot of money on taxes and protect one's assets from creditors. Afterwards I decided to take the plunge and buy a whole life insurance policy in a tax haven. The money invested in the policy started to build my multi-family property portfolio.

The Importance of Protecting Your Wealth

As you become more successful, you will likely start to accumulate more wealth. This is a good thing, but it also comes with some challenges. One of the biggest challenges is protecting your wealth from unnecessary taxation. The government taxes income, capital gains, and even wealth transfers (such as inheritances). The more wealth you have, the more taxes you will pay. This can be a significant drain on your resources, and it can make it difficult to grow your wealth over time.

Strategies for Protecting Your Wealth

There are several strategies you can use to protect your wealth from taxation. Some of the most common strategies include:

Investing in tax-deferred accounts:

There are several tax-deferred investment accounts available, such as 401(k)s, IRAs, and HSAs. These accounts allow you to grow your wealth tax-deferred, which can save you a significant amount of money over time.

Using insurance products:

There are a few insurance products that can be used to protect your wealth from taxation. Whole life insurance is one example. Whole life insurance policies build cash value over time, and this cash value can be borrowed from tax-free.

Reducing your taxable income: There are a few ways to reduce your taxable income. Some of the most common ways include:

- Deducting business expenses

- Deducting medical expenses

- Deducting charitable contributions

- Taking advantage of tax credits

Leverage Whole Life Insurance as a Borrowing Device

Whole life insurance is a type of permanent life insurance that provides both death benefit and cash value. The cash value grows tax-deferred, and it can be borrowed from tax-free.

Borrowing from your whole life insurance policy can be a great way to access your wealth without having to pay taxes. The interest you pay on the loan is typically lower than the interest you would pay on a credit card or other loan, and you can repay the loan at any time without penalty.

THE BREAKDOWN:

Protecting your wealth from unnecessary taxation is an important part of financial planning. There are a few strategies you can use to do so, including investing in tax-deferred accounts, using insurance products, and reducing your taxable income.

Leverage whole life insurance as a borrowing device can be a great way to access your wealth without having to pay taxes. The interest you pay on the loan is typically lower than the interest you would pay on a credit card or other loan, and you can repay the loan at any time without penalty.

The rich use life insurance products to avoid taxes in several ways. Here are a few examples:

Using life insurance to pay estate taxes.

The estate tax is a tax that is imposed on the transfer of assets at death. The amount of the estate tax is based on the value of the estate, and the current exemption is $12.92 million for individuals and $25.84 million for couples. If a person's estate is worth more than the exemption, the estate tax will be due. Life insurance can be used to pay estate taxes by naming the estate as the beneficiary of the policy. When the insured person dies, the insurance company will pay the death benefit to the estate, which can then use the money to pay the estate tax bill.

Using life insurance to create a tax-free legacy.

The death benefit of a life insurance policy is not subject to income tax. This means that if a wealthy person leaves their life insurance policy to their heirs, the heirs will not have to pay income tax on the money. This can be a valuable way to create a tax-free legacy for the wealthy. For example, a wealthy person could leave their life insurance policy to their children, who could then use the money to pay for college, a down payment on a house, or other expenses.

Using life insurance to protect assets from creditors.

Life insurance proceeds are generally protected from creditors. This means that if a wealthy person is sued or goes bankrupt, their creditors cannot take their life insurance policy. This can be a valuable way to protect assets from creditors. For example, a wealthy person could take out a life insurance policy on themselves and name their spouse as the beneficiary. If the wealthy person were to die, their spouse would receive the death benefit, which would be protected from creditors.

Using life insurance to save on taxes.

Life insurance can be used to save on taxes in several ways. For example, the premiums paid on a life insurance policy can be tax-deductible, and the growth of the cash value of a life insurance policy can be tax deferred. This can be a valuable way to save on taxes for the wealthy. For example, a wealthy person could take out a whole life insurance policy and deduct the premiums from their taxable income. The cash value of the policy would grow tax-deferred, and the death benefit would be paid out tax-free.

It is important to note that life insurance is not a tax shelter. The benefits of life insurance can be used to reduce taxes, but they cannot eliminate them. For example, if a wealthy person leaves their life insurance policy to their heirs, the heirs will still have to pay estate taxes on the death benefit. However, life insurance can be a valuable tool for the wealthy to use to reduce their tax liability. When used properly, life insurance can help the wealthy to protect their assets, save on taxes, and create a tax-free legacy.

LESSON NO. 22
SELF-MADE TASTES BETTER

REAL ESTATE OWNERSHIP is a cornerstone to wealth generation. Over time, real estate tends to appreciate, which can provide significant financial gains for homeowners. Additionally, real estate can generate income through rent payments, which can further increase wealth. There are many historical examples of people who have amassed great wealth through real estate. For example, John D. Rockefeller, the founder of Standard Oil, is said to have made his fortune through real estate investments. He owned a large portfolio of properties in New York City, which appreciated significantly in value over time. Recently, there are many millionaires and billionaires who have acquired their fortunes through real estate. For example, Sam Zell, the chairman of Equity Group Investments, is a self-made billionaire who made his fortune through real estate investments. He has owned and managed a large portfolio of properties, including office buildings, hotels, and apartment complexes.

Real estate can be a great way to build wealth, but it is important to do your research and make sure you are investing in the right properties. There are many factors to consider when investing in real estate, such as location, property type, and rental demand. If you are considering investing in real estate, it is important to consult with a financial advisor to get personalized advice.

Here are some additional tips for building wealth through real estate:

- Start early: The earlier you start investing in real estate, the more time your investments must grow.

- Invest in properties that are in good locations: Properties in desirable locations are more likely to appreciate over time.

- Consider investing in rental properties: Rental properties can generate income, which can help you to pay off your mortgage and build wealth.

- Diversify your portfolio. Don't invest all your money in one property. Spread your money out over several properties to reduce your risk.

- Be patient. Real estate investing is a long-term investment. Don't expect to get rich quick.

If you are willing to put in the work, real estate can be a great way to build wealth and achieve financial security. There are a few ways to get real estate financing without a working income, if you are self-employed. Here are a few options:

- Get a co-signer. A co-signer is someone who agrees to be responsible for the loan if you can't make payments. This can be a good option if you have good credit but don't have a lot of income.

- Get a portfolio loan. A portfolio loan is a type of loan that is not insured by the government. This means that the lender takes on more risk, but they may also be willing to lend to borrowers who don't have traditional income.

- Get a hard money loan. A hard money loan is a type of short-term loan that is secured by real estate. These loans typically have higher interest rates and fees, but they can be a good option if you need money quickly.

- Get a private loan. A private loan is a loan that is made by an individual or a group of individuals. These loans can be arranged through friends, family, or other investors.

THE BREAKDOWN:

It is important to note that getting real estate financing without a working income can be more difficult than getting a loan with a traditional income. You will need to have good credit and a strong financial history. You will also need to be able to show the lender that you could make the monthly payments. If you are self-employed and you are considering buying real estate, it is important to talk to a lender to see what options are available to you. There are a few ways to leverage an LLC, C-Corps/S-corps to take advantage of a multi-unit property loan by living in one unit and collecting rents simultaneously from the other units. One way is to form an LLC or corporation and then take out a loan in the name of the entity. This can help to protect your personal assets in case of default on the loan. Additionally, lenders may be more willing to lend to an LLC or corporation than to an individual, especially if you have a limited credit history.

Another way to leverage an LLC, C-Corps/S-corps is to use it to qualify for a loan with a lower interest rate. This is because lenders often offer lower interest rates to businesses than to individuals. Additionally, businesses may be able to deduct certain expenses related to the property, such as property taxes and insurance, which can further reduce the cost of ownership. Finally, you can use an LLC, C-Corps/S-corps to structure your ownership of the property in a way that minimizes your tax liability. For example, you may be able to deduct the mortgage interest and property taxes on your personal tax return if you live in one of the units and rent out the others. Additionally, you may be able to defer capital gains taxes on the sale of the property if you hold it for at least 10 years.

Here are some additional tips for leveraging an LLC, C-Corps/S-corps to take advantage of a multi-unit property loan:

- Make sure you understand the tax implications of owning a property through an entity.

- Get professional advice from an accountant or attorney before forming an entity.

- Make sure you have a clear understanding of the terms of the loan before you sign it.

THE BREAKDOWN:

It is important to note that there are some drawbacks to using an LLC, C-Corps/S-corps, to take advantage of a multi-unit property loan. For example, you will have to pay additional fees to form and maintain the entity. Additionally, you will have to file additional tax returns for the entity. Overall, there are several ways to leverage an LLC, C-Corps/S-corps to take advantage of a multi-unit property loan. However, it is important to weigh the pros and cons carefully before deciding.

LESSON NO. 23
GHOST MODE

Solitude's advantage:
"A retreat to recalibrate, sharpen focus, and strategize in the silence of mastery."

—BUILD

I N THE WORLD of trading, there is a saying that goes, "If you're not cheating, you're not trying." This is because the market is constantly changing and evolving, and in order to stay ahead of the curve, you need to be willing to do whatever it takes.

One of the most powerful tools that you can use to your advantage is ghost mode. Ghost mode is a state of being where you completely remove yourself from the market and focus on your own personal development. This means no charts, no news, and no social media. When you're in ghost mode, you're able to clear your head and focus on what's important. You're able to identify your weaknesses and develop a plan to improve them. You're also able to come up with new trading strategies that are tailored to your own personality and style. Going into ghost mode can be a scary proposition. After all, you're essentially giving up control of your trading. But if you're willing to take the risk, you'll be rewarded with a much deeper understanding of the market and a much more powerful trading edge.

Here are a few tips for going into ghost mode:

- Set a goal. What do you want to achieve by going into ghost mode? Do you want to develop a new trading strategy? Do you want to improve your risk management? Once you know what you want to achieve, you can start to develop a plan.

- Remove yourself from the market. This means no charts, no news, and no social media. Anything that could potentially distract you from your goals should be eliminated.

- Focus on your personal development. This is your time to improve yourself as a trader. Read books, watch videos, and talk to other traders. The more you learn, the better you'll become.

- Be patient. It takes time to develop a new trading edge. Don't expect to see results overnight. Just keep working hard and you'll eventually reach your goals.

- Going into ghost mode is not for everyone. But if you're willing to put in the work, it can be a very rewarding experience. By taking a step back from the market and focusing on your own personal development, you'll be able to come back stronger than ever before.

If you want to be a successful trader, you need to be willing to do whatever it takes. That includes going into ghost mode from time to time. Ghost mode is a state of being where you completely remove yourself from the market and focus on your own personal development. This means no charts, no news, and no social media. When you're in ghost mode, you're able to clear your head and focus on what's important. You're able to identify your weaknesses and develop a plan to improve them. You're also able to come up with new trading strategies that are tailored to your own personality and style.

Going into ghost mode can be a scary proposition. After all, you're essentially giving up control of your trading. But if you're willing to take the risk, you'll be rewarded with a much deeper understanding of the market and a much more powerful trading edge.

So if you're serious about becoming a successful trader, I encourage you to consider going into ghost mode. It's one of the most powerful tools that you can use to your advantage.

Benefits of taking time to collect thoughts prior to making a move:

- It can help you to make better decisions. When you take the time to collect your thoughts, you can think more clearly and rationally. This can help you to identify the best course of action and avoid making impulsive decisions.

- It can help you to avoid making mistakes. When you decide without taking the time to think it through, you are more likely to make a mistake. Taking the time to collect your thoughts can help you to identify potential risks and avoid making costly mistakes.

- It can help you to stay calm and focused. When you are faced with a difficult decision, it can be easy to get overwhelmed and make rash decisions. Taking the time to collect your thoughts can help you to stay calm and focused, which can lead to better decision-making.

These benefits can be applied to investing, real estate investing, and business. In all these areas, it is important to make sound decisions that are based on careful analysis. By taking the time to collect your thoughts, you can increase your chances of making wise decisions that will lead to success.

Here are some specific examples of how taking time to collect thoughts can benefit you in these areas:

Investing: When you are considering investing in a particular stock or mutual fund, it is important to do your research and understand the risks involved. Taking the time to collect your thoughts can help you to make an informed decision about whether to invest.

Real estate investing: When you are considering buying a rental property, it is important to assess the property's potential for income and expenses. Taking the time to collect your thoughts can help you to make a wise investment decision.

Business: When you are starting a business, it is important to have a clear plan and strategy. Taking the time to collect your thoughts can help you to develop a sound business plan that will increase your chances of success.

THE BREAKDOWN:

Taking the time to collect thoughts prior to making a move can have many benefits. By taking the time to think things through, you can increase your chances of making wise decisions that will lead to success.

LESSON NO. 24
YOU'RE ALWAYS BUILDING...
EVEN WHEN BROKE

"Wealth flows freely. Abundance is my birthright.
Prosperity knows no bounds."

– BUILD

IN THE REALM of personal finance, there's a force that works tirelessly in your favor: the power of compounding. It's a game-changer, my friends. Allow me to break it down for you in the language of...Picture this: You toss a humble $100 into an investment, and it earns you a 10% return. Boom! You now have $110. But wait, it gets even better. That 10% was not just pocketed; it's reinvested. So, my savvy comrades, your $110 earns another 10%, racking up a total of $120. This is the beauty of compounding—interest on interest, baby.

And the plot thickens. Year after year, your investment keeps growing faster and faster. It's like a snowball rolling downhill, gaining momentum. That $120 earns another 10%, a cool $12, bringing your total investment to $132. See how it multiplies? This is where the magic happens.

But here's the kicker: the longer you invest, the sweeter the payoff. Imagine investing a mere $100 per month for 30 years, with an average annual return of 7%. Brace yourself, my friends, for the mind-blowing truth. At the end of those three decades, your investment would be worth a staggering six-figure sum— over $100,000! And it all started with those humble Benjamin Franklins.

Now, don't be discouraged if your pockets feel light. The beauty of compounding is that it works for everyone, regardless of your current financial status. You just need to act. Start early and save regularly, even if it's spare change. Every little bit count, my comrades.

So, let me drop some wisdom on you. Here's an exercise to turn your spare change into a fortune of dividend stocks:

Step one:

Set up a separate bank account, solely dedicated to your investment money. Keep it separate, my friends, for clarity and focus.

Step two:

Embrace the art of rounding up. Every time you make a purchase, round up to the nearest dollar and deposit the difference into your investment account. Those small amounts will snowball into something significant, trust me.

Step three:

Channel your inner mogul and invest your hard-earned money into a diversified portfolio of dividend stocks. Spread the risk, my friends, and let those dividends rain down.

Step four:

The power moves—reinvest those dividends. Let them increase your investment even faster. This is how fortunes are forged, my comrades.

By following these steps, you're building wealth from the ground up, even when you feel financially constrained. The power of compounding is your ally, relentlessly working in your favor. So, embrace it, harness it, and let it propel you toward the life of abundance you deserve. Remember, you're always building brick by brick, dollar by dollar. The path to prosperity starts with that first investment, no matter how humble. Now go forth and conquer the world of compounding, my comrades. The throne of wealth awaits your arrival.

Get them started early (teaching the children):

The realm of financial wisdom extends even to our little successors. Let's dive into the world of custodial IRAs, a path paved with potential riches for our young prodigies.

Picture this: a custodial IRA, a vehicle that allows parents or guardians to open an individual retirement account on behalf of their children. It's like planting a seed of financial independence in fertile soil. As the custodian, you hold the reins, guiding and nurturing their financial future.

Now, you might wonder, "When is the optimal age to embark on this journey?" Well, my friends, the answer lies in the sweet spot between innocence and maturity. As soon as your child starts earning income through part-time jobs, gigs, or even their entrepreneurial ventures, it's time to seize the opportunity.

Why, you ask? Because the power of time is our greatest ally in the realm of investing. The earlier we sow the seeds of financial knowledge, the longer they must grow and compound. By starting early, we grant their investments ample time to weather market storms and emerge victorious.

Imagine the potential, my comrades. Let's say a young protégé earns a modest income during their teenage years. Instead of splurging on fleeting pleasures (use your imagination), they contribute a portion of their earnings to a custodial IRA. Now, fast forward a few decades. That small investment, nurtured by compounding returns and the magic of time, has blossomed into a substantial retirement fund. But remember, the custodial IRA is not merely about amassing wealth. It's an opportunity to teach our youth about financial responsibility, the art of investing, and the importance of preparing for the future. So, seize the moment. Open the doors to a custodial IRA for your children at the optimal age, when they begin earning income. Nurture their financial journey, educate them on the power of compounding, and watch them embark on a path toward financial independence.

Slow Rollin to the bank

The Oracle of Omaha, the legendary Warren Buffett. A name that resonates with power, wisdom, and boundless wealth. Let's delve into the realm of dividends and unveil the annual treasure trove that flows into Buffett's coffers.

In the year 2022, my astute comrades, Warren Buffett, the sage of investing, reveled in a bountiful harvest of dividends. We're talking about those glorious payouts bestowed upon shareholders by the companies they invest in. It's the sound of money raining down, a symphony of wealth echoing through the halls of the investing elite. Now, you might wonder, just how much did our Wall Street titan earn in dividends during that illustrious year? Brace yourselves for the staggering truth. Hold onto your seats, my friends, for the numbers we're about to unveil shall surely ignite your ambition.

Warren Buffett, the master of compounding, witnessed his dividend income surge to the tune of billions. Yes, you heard that right—billions. We're talking about the kind of wealth that can move mountains, the kind of dividends that could reshape nations.

While the precise figures for 2022 may elude us at this moment, we can gaze upon the previous years as a testament to Buffett's dividend prowess. In 2021, the Oracle of Omaha raked in a mind-boggling $3.8 billion in dividends. Yes, my comrades, that's billions with a "B." It's the kind of money that could buy you entire companies, or perhaps an exotic island or two.

But let us not be captivated by the numbers alone. The true essence of Buffett's dividend kingdom lies in the power of his strategic investments. He carefully selects companies with robust business models, stable earnings, and a commitment to rewarding shareholders through dividends. Warren Buffett understands the beauty of passive income, the art of making money while you sleep. He knows that dividends are the secret weapon in an investor's arsenal, the fuel that propels wealth creation on autopilot.

So, my ambitious builders, take a page from Buffett's playbook. Embrace the world of dividends, where your investments shower you with a steady stream of income. Just remember, it's not only about the dollars and cents—it's about the knowledge, the strategy, and the long-term vision that drives the Oracle's dividend empire.

LESSON NO. 25
TEN TOES DOWN

LESSON No. 25, brings us to the sacred ground of unwavering discipline.
The cornerstone of success, the secret sauce that separates the winners from the losers. Listen closely, for I shall reveal the power that lies within the realm of "ten toes down" commitment. In this tumultuous game we call life, consistency reigns supreme. It is the battle cry of the disciplined, the resolute BUILDERS who refuse to surrender to their whims and desires. Discipline demands that we persevere, that we push through the barriers that stand in our path. It is a relentless pursuit of greatness, fueled by a burning desire to achieve more than our egos dare to dream. Let us not be blinded by the allure of discipline without understanding its duality. For every coin has two sides, and discipline is no exception. Allow me to illuminate the pros and cons of this

purposeful stubbornness, this unwavering commitment to our chosen path.

The pros of discipline are as bright as the morning sun. With discipline by our side, we gain the power of consistency. We forge a habit of excellence, where each action builds upon the next, creating a foundation for success. We become masters of our craft, refining our skills day after day, unyielding in our pursuit of mastery. And with discipline as our ally, we unleash the full force of our potential, achieving heights that mere mortals can only dream of.

Yet, let us not forget the shadow that looms over discipline—the cons that we must face. Discipline demands sacrifice. It requires us to forsake the pleasures of instant gratification, to endure the discomfort of delayed rewards. It challenges our resolve, tempting us with shortcuts and distractions. It whispers doubts and tests our commitment. But fear not, for those who understand the power of discipline will rise above these obstacles, emerging stronger and more resilient. So, embrace the power of discipline. Let it be your guiding light on this treacherous journey. Fuel your actions with a purpose that surpasses the petty roadblocks that attempt to impede your progress. Find your why, your driving force, and let it propel you forward with unwavering determination. Remember, discipline is not for the faint of the heart. It is for the fearless, the unyielding, the tenacious. It is the mark of a true BUILDER, and it is within your grasp. So, stand tall, my comrades, plant those ten toes firmly on the ground, and let the power of discipline carry you to the pinnacle of success.

Repetition is the key to compound growth. It is the secret weapon that propels us towards greatness. So, let us be disciplined, let us be consistent, and let us harness the power of repetition to transform ourselves into the best versions of who we can be. Now, go and trade in the currency of repetition, and watch as the dividends of your self-improvement compound before your very eyes. The delicate dance between a winning streak and a losing slump. In the ever-changing tides of the financial arena, we witness the ebb and flow of fortune. It is in these moments that we must navigate with a keen eye and a steady hand, for the difference between the two is like night and day.

During a winning streak, the winds of success are at our backs. We ride the waves of triumph, executing our strategies flawlessly and reaping the rewards. Confidence courses through our veins, and every decision seems to lead to prosperity. The market dances to our tune, and we revel in the sweet taste of victory. But let us not be deceived, for the ebb is an inevitable companion to the flow. In the face of a losing slump, the tides turn against us. The market becomes a tempestuous sea, filled with uncertainty and volatility. Our once-reliable strategies falter, and losses pile up like crashing waves. Doubt creeps in, and we find ourselves questioning our abilities.

In these moments, the true test of a BUILDER emerges. A winning streak may inflate our ego, tempting us to believe we are invincible. But it is in the depths of a losing slump that our resilience and mental fortitude are truly put to the test. It is here that we must summon the strength to rise above adversity, to learn from our mistakes, and to adapt our strategies. The key lies in our response to these ebbs and flows. A winning streak should not be a cause for complacency or recklessness, but rather an opportunity for self-reflection and improvement. It is during these times that we must remain disciplined and focused, diligently analyzing our successes to replicate them in the future. When faced with a losing slump, we must resist the temptation to despair or abandon ship. Instead, we must embrace the challenge, knowing that it is in these difficult moments that true growth occurs. We must adjust our sails, refine our strategies, and approach the market with renewed determination.

Remember, that the ebb and flow of the market is a natural phenomenon. Just as the ocean tides rise and fall, so does the financial landscape. It is our ability to adapt, to weather the storms, and to seize the opportunities that sets us apart as BUILDERS.

So, when the winds of fortune shift, and you find yourself amid a winning streak or a losing slump, remain steadfast. Learn from the victories, humbly acknowledge the defeats, and always strive to improve. For it is in the ebb and flow that the true art of the game reveals itself. Let me enlighten you on the profound simplicity of repetition and its undeniable impact on our journey to success. In the realm of finance, we witness the magic of compounding growth through dividend stock trading. But let us not underestimate the power of repetition in our daily self-improvement endeavors. Just as in the world of trading, where consistent investments in dividend stocks yield compound returns over time, so too does the habit of repetition in our personal growth. It is through the consistent repetition of positive actions, my comrades, that we unlock the gates to exponential progress.

Imagine, if you will, the beauty of compound growth in our daily lives. Each day, we commit ourselves to small yet meaningful acts of self-improvement. We engage in rituals that sharpen our minds, strengthen our bodies, and nurture our souls. Like a skilled investor reinvesting dividend, we reinvest our efforts into our personal growth, compounding the benefits day after day. With each repetition, we inch closer to our desired outcomes. We sharpen our skills, expand our knowledge, and refine our character. We accumulate wisdom, resilience, and an unwavering mindset. Just as the power of compound interest amplifies our wealth, the power of repetition amplifies our growth, propelling us to new heights.

Let us not forget the comparison, just as dividend stock trading requires discipline and consistency, so does our journey of self-improvement. We must remain steadfast in our commitment, unwavering in our pursuit of growth. We must resist the temptations of complacency and instant gratification, for it is in the power of repetition that we find our true strength. So, let us embrace the power of repetition in our quest for self-improvement. Let us cultivate daily rituals that nourish our minds, bodies, and spirits. Let us remember that the accumulation of small, consistent efforts yields extraordinary results. Just as the dividends from wise investments grow exponentially, so too shall our personal growth flourish.

LESSON NO. 26
EPILOGUE

BUILD OR DESTROY Vol. 2 has come to an end. But the lessons within these pages are just the beginning.

If you've read this far, then you've already taken the first step on your journey to becoming a builder. You've learned about the importance of making friends with pain, the power of affirmations, the power of gratitude, and the strength of bonds. You've learned about influence, the importance of teaching children, the power of community, the importance of developing patience, remaining stoic, leveraging the LLC or C-Corp/S-Corp, the importance of skilled trades, the importance of good credit, the leverage of stack investment, tapping into your birthright (hidden potential), putting in the work yesterday, resetting the game, the power of indifference, costly habits and bad investments, leveraging your methods - unlocking your natural talents, mentorship for hire - unlocking the power of guidance, protecting the bag, at all cost, self-made tastes better, ghost mode, you're always building...even when broke, and remaining ten toes down.

These are just the basics. There is so much more to learn about building, and the best way to learn is by doing. So, get out there and start. Start by taking one small step at a time without the fear of failure. Remember, it's all a part of the process. It's how we learn and grow. The most important thing is to never give up. Keep Griding, keep learning, and keep growing. And eventually, you will achieve your goals.

Here are some reasons why it's important to bet on yourself:

- You are the only one who can control your destiny. No one else is going to make your dreams come true for you. You must be the one to take the risks, put in the work, and make the sacrifices.

- You have nothing to lose. If you fail, you'll learn from your mistakes and come back stronger. But if you don't even try, you'll never know what you could have achieved.

- You owe it to yourself to live your best life. You only have one life to live, so you should make the most of it. If you have a dream, you should go for it. You don't want to look back on your life and regret not taking a chance.

- You're still young and able-bodied. This is the time in your life when you have the most energy and drive. You're also less likely to have responsibilities like a family or a mortgage. So now is the time to take risks and go after your dreams.

Here are some reasons why you owe it to yourself to take a chance while you're still young and able-bodied:

- You'll have more energy and drive. As you get older, you'll have less energy and drive. So, it's important to take advantage of your youth and go after your dreams while you still have the energy to do it.

- You'll be less likely to have responsibilities. If you wait until you're older to take a chance, you'll likely have more responsibilities, like a family or a mortgage. These responsibilities can make it more difficult to take risks and go after your dreams.

- You have less to lose. If you fail when you're young, you'll have less to lose. You'll still have time to recover and try again. But if you wait until you're older to fail, it will be more difficult to recover.

So, if you have a dream, don't wait. Go for it now while you're still young and able-bodied. You owe it to yourself to live your best life…You are a builder.